Five
ANALOGIES
for
FICTION
writing

GW00670440

Sam North

TWENTIETH CENTURY

Gylphi
ARTS &
HUMANITIES
PUBLISHER

AND BEYOND

A *Gylphi Limited* Book

First published in Great Britain in 2012
by Gylphi Limited

A CIP catalogue record for this book is available from the British Library.

ISBN 978-1-78024-006-0 (pbk)

Cover design and typesetting by Gylphi Limited.
Printed in the UK by MPG Biddles Ltd, Norfolk.

Gylphi Limited
PO Box 993
Canterbury CT1 9EP
UK

CONTENTS

INTRODUCTION

We want to write a novel and we desire passionately the object itself, our book, whether its cover will be red-and-black with a gold embossed title, or a tasteful apricot with a sepia print of an old townscape, or maybe it will have no physical covers or pages and be an eBook; whichever is the case we *will* write it, for the glory, and the chance to make a killing, and because we have a *theory* of some description. We are here, at this moment: you and I want to be a novelist, or a novelist again.

In my case, I have a head start — or perhaps it is a false start — because I composed a sequence in a previous novel that I cut out; it had queered the story. Red lines were scored through twenty or more pages, but even as I took the chunk of A4 paper, neatly dented by my thumb, and inserted it into the pink-rimmed, painted metal bucket that seems to serve as the waste for all my most beautiful phrases and powerful ideas, I became determined not to throw it away, but instead to grow it into a novel on its own account. Block on, cut, new document, paste. This is what I start with now, a file named *What The Children Saw*.

The big questions arise immediately. How shall we write — or *make* — our novels beautifully? Which are the levers to pull, where are the trapdoors?

Writing exercise no. 1: 'Wurge'

Don't think about your book or your writing. Merely write a 'wurge' — that is, a splurge of words — but in this case, make all of them concrete nouns.

Concrete nouns (desk, motor car, rabbit) are powerful words because they describe objects that are tangible to all our senses; most especially they conjure images which can be observed by our primary sense — sight. It's pertinent that the word 'image' is contained in the word 'imagination'. If we were asked to write a novel that was to be read only by moles, we would concentrate primarily on scent not image.

Take a familiar routine that you don't have to think about, like driving to work or feeding your pet cat or arriving home. Set an alarm and write without stopping and without thinking for one whole minute, but *using only concrete nouns.* You won't have to think about composition, but you will have to inhabit your mind's eye and live the sequence of events and deliver that vision directly and precisely to the page.

To begin with, we might have an empty sheet of paper waiting under the stiff cover of a notebook, and we might write by hand; or we might head straight for the computer keyboard. One novelist I know composes the outlines of his novels while standing at an easel. We have some early thoughts and ideas, and a more or less ongoing piece of time ... and, most of all, we have ambition. In addition, we have other writers to look to: we write on the proverbial school desk, scratched with the names of those who have written before us.

E. M. Forster, in *Aspects of the Novel* (1927), conjured an image of all novelists, throughout time, writing in the same room while he looked over their shoulders to read their compositions. He invited H. G. Wells to sit next to Dickens, Samuel Richardson to be near Henry James, and he advised them — you are alike, in a way.

Many more writers have entered Forster's room-of-all-writers since he first suggested it in 1927, and they have all been examined and written about. I want to use some of them to cut a swathe through this process of novel-writing and understand how it is done.

In order to do so, I have extended and thoroughly beat out five analogies: The Burn, The Alchemist, The Invasion, The Donkey's

Head and The Constant Gardener. All the while aware that analogies, no matter how picturesque or entertaining, can be an imperfect way of describing concepts: they possess a hallucinatory quality that can be misleading, and to stick within the confines of an analogy will restrict what is permitted.

However, in expounding the analogies, I believe the form proves itself. This is because the use of analogy creates an exploratory method; it is a way of travelling, and in that sense (as Seamus Heaney describes poetic form), it is 'both the ship and the anchor' (Heaney, 1996: 29).

1. THE BURN

On entering Forster's room-of-all-writers, one thing is immediately evident: the inhabitants have an abundance of intellectual energy. They need it. To write a novel is an exercise in concentration. If we are going to deploy such effort over many months or years, the prerequisite is a sufficiently strong desire to complete the task — motivation-as-fuel. Pick up a good book and weigh it in your hand. You can smell the exhaust trail of the distinct types of fuel used in writing it. The reader is typically able to detect the root of the writer's motivation, where it started, and how it kept going.

In any event, the fuel must be burned to good effect. My cousin by marriage, Mike McHugh Junior, recently fitted out a floating oil rig in the Teesside ship-building yards. It was an enormous structure. Our task should be as spectacular and as large-scale an operation. But first we need to find fuel, pump it ashore and store it, because we have a long and arduous task in front of us burning up the word count, writing this novel.

The word 'burn' calls to mind the acceleration of a rocket, or muscles strained in exertion. However, there are slow burns as well: a candle, and the hand-warmer I was given during a childhood ski-trip that smouldered in a drawstring velvet pouch in my pocket. Most works of fiction accelerate into the literary firmament using a variety of fuels. This means that if we think of a book as having a single engine, the analogy immediately risks not making sense. It is necessary to think instead of the novel as more akin to a hybrid car, something that contains at least two types of engine.

My ambition is to write a story called *What The Children Saw* and it would help me to wander through Forster's room and group these other writers according to what type of fuel is burning in them. If, in other words, I analyse their various motivations (beyond the three motivations common to all writers: glory, money and that *theory*) and ask myself which group or groups would welcome me? In whose company would I find myself most comfortable?

1. The political motive

Most writers have a world view — a *theory* — that is embedded in their writing; and in that sense most writers are political with a small 'p'. The kind of writer I will be discussing in the next few pages goes beyond that; they want to change the political map.

While running a finger along my bookshelves, I stop because Lara Santoro is next to George Orwell. It is precisely how Forster would have placed them. Orwell claimed it was history that turned him into a political writer; he felt that he lived in an age which, in its political violence, prescribed such a course for him. Lara Santoro, in her novel *Mercy* (2007), also writes with a political agenda.

With Orwell and Lara Santoro already in hand, I pull out Bertolt Brecht and then Indra Sinha from the shelves, because all are burning the same type of fuel: their work has been motivated by a desire to foster political change.

They stare out at the reader from their author photographs with courage, but they are also hurt. They have a passionate, yearning look. Their work is urgent too, purposeful and directed at every man, woman and child. You can hear the roar of right and wrong. Lara Santoro's novel, *Mercy*, calls for that eponymous virtue to be the guiding sponsor in our dealings with AIDS sufferers in Nairobi and she pins the whole extent of her novel to the lines from Paul's First Letter to the Corinthians, which she quotes at the very end, by which time we are on our knees with agreement. '*Though I have mastered the tongues of men and angels, and have not mercy, I am like sounding brass or crashing cymbal. ... And though I give all my goods to feed the poor, and my body to be burned, and have not mercy, I am nothing*' (Santoro, 2007: 277). Yes. We will and should change.

Santoro signals her motivation in a significant twist she gives to her translation of Paul's First Letter to the Corinthians. The passage — as quoted in her pages — reads: ' ... and have not mercy ... '. English translations of the New Testament have typically translated the original Greek word used by Paul in this epistle, '*charitas*', as 'love'. Others (including the King James version of 1611) have diluted the force of Paul's original words by less accurately translating the word as 'charity'.

Santoro's slight but careful alteration from 'love' or 'charity' to 'mercy' reveals a telling change of emphasis. The novel *Mercy* is itself a work that passionately sets out to show its readers that the quality of mercy — a quality that is embodied in the narrative in the larger-than-life figure of the woman named Mercy, can be defined as love made evident in *action*. The urgency of Santoro's message insists that what is called for, when faced with the scale of such catastrophes as AIDS, be they natural or man-made, is neither outrage, nor disgust, nor unproductive anger, nor even some abstract principle or simple attitude of love; rather, such catastrophes must be met with love in the form of its lived and embodied human capacity for active and transformative compassion.

By means of a single, subtle change in her closing epigraph, the novel's emphasis is made all the more clear. We too can and must change our ways if we are ever to begin to meet such crises. The quality of our own mercy itself 'an attribute of God', as Shakespeare reminded us through the character of Portia centuries before, must not ever be strained in a world such as ours.

The authorial motive that is powered by raw political passion is a fuel that has not burned all that brightly among those writers who have worked within the Anglophone traditions of fiction. One reason might be that the kinds of issues that these novels tend to confront have been dealt with in the still-strong and muscular forms of non-fiction, journalism, and reportage that have developed side-by-side with those of fiction in the patterns and traditions of narrative in the western world. It is no accident, therefore, that all my chosen novelists were or are engaged to a greater or lesser extent with journalism.

Orwell's rough tweed jacket and trousers were perfectly the style in Orwell's own lifetime, when populist forms of Socialism and Communism flourished throughout Britain. Movements of the British Left that embraced everyone from Clement Attlee to the likes of Stephen Spender, J. B. S. Haldane, and Orwell himself, and that were embodied in left-wing institutions such as the Left Book Club (which provides for Orwell a perfect setting for one of the key scenes in his novel, *Coming Up for Air* [1939]) found themselves massed on one side of an ideological divide, pitted against a monolithic and exploitative Capitalism. In the picture that sits in front of me, Orwell has been caught by the camera in the homely act of lighting his pipe, yet the horrors of the Great War lie just beyond the edge of historical memory, and, just beyond the living borders of the picture's frame, even more inconceivable atrocities are still to come. Such awareness gilds the photo, for the modern viewer, with an unpreventable sense of loss. With such awareness, with such knowledge, comes the horror that Joseph Conrad had glimpsed, as if by flashes of lightning, in *Heart of Darkness*; the horror of the kind that Orwell himself was himself to experience and to capture so well not by the flash of lightning, but by something more comparable to the unbearable torment of a looped film clip that is destined to repeat without end.

Orwell made his own list of writerly motivations in 'Why I Write' (1946/2000). He defines his own motivation unequivocally: 'Every line of serious work that I have written since 1936 has been written, directly or indirectly, against totalitarianism and for democratic socialism as I understand it' (Orwell, 1946/2000: 5). It is obvious in photographs, in articles and essays, in the happenstance of his life, in his books, and that is why he burned.

My desire to be among this group is powerful because the books are important; they aim to affect the surge and sway of events. Can I stay here, among this group? I even have a jacket like Orwell's, and trousers similar, and the sensible shoes. I never wear them. I would like to have gone to such lengths as he did to purify his ambition. He was born into the English ruling class but disliked their manners, and his dismay was sharpened by Eton, class of 1917. I also disliked the public school to which I won a bursary and left for the local comprehensive. Orwell deliberately descended into poverty for two years in Paris in order to explore the conditions faced by an enslaved working class (*Down and Out in Paris and London* [1933]). In my case, it was rather out of necessity than an ambition to experience the deprivations of the proletariat that I worked on building sites and in factories from the age of 16 to 28. Orwell's desire was to immerse himself in the political lot of man. Mine was to escape it.

I went on to work for television companies and literary agencies and grew to weigh thirteen stone; Orwell was part of the left-wing volunteer exodus to fight against Franco in Spain, became so thin his ribs showed, and was shot in the neck. He became editor of *Tribune*, the socialist magazine, and wrote in its pages for years. I latched onto the coat tails of two famous men to ghostwrite bestsellers.

Orwell's factual writings were a prelude to the great works of fiction when he came off the ramparts to warn us of how communism transmogrified into totalitarianism in *Animal Farm*, a fable that castigates the Russian revolution and the factional in-fighting that he witnessed in Barcelona when he had to hide, and run for his life, from his own side. He invented a model of what a totalitarian state might look like for us in *Nineteen Eighty-Four*. His disillusionment in foretelling the rise of Fascism and the Second World War and in witnessing the totalitarianism that infected the Socialist cause harked back to his original finding in *The Road to Wigan Pier*, that 'All government is evil … that the punishment' (Orwell, 1937/2001: 107). In the end Orwell entered an asylum, burnt out.

My novels (while I am inspired to make them compelling to others) are personal explorations of ideas that seem important to me, but are not political ideas. I wish to better myself more than I wish to improve the lot of my fellow man; I live in a lovely house with a wife and children; I cultivate sanity and wish to amass happiness, develop it, turn it to my account.

I do not think I belong here. Next to Orwell stands instead of me Indra Sinha, living and working in France in the present day; or, rather he crouches, because he has with him his dog, Holly, an old English sheepdog. Sinha's silver, bouffant hair and kindly but determined eyes give him a similar look to Holly's, although he is heavier in the face.

Sinha gave a sustained commitment over a period of many years to the town of Bhopal, and wrote a novel, *Animal's People* (2007), which sprang from it. The novel has a passionate, sensual connection with language and emotion that suggests it will not be only here, in this group with Orwell, that I will find Sinha. Nevertheless, he can hold his head up in this company.

He was born in India, educated in England, and significantly (after the BBC had turned him down as a documentary film-maker) worked in advertising. The pattern is similar to that of Salman Rushdie's life. He happened to write an advertisement for Amnesty and consequently, since 1993, has campaigned to help the citizens of Bhopal, the town which in 1984 was poisoned by a gas escape from a chemical factory owned by the US corporate giant Union Carbide. The leak killed between 8,000 and 15,000 people. Union Carbide refused to clean up. Citizens were offered 500 dollars each in compensation. Sinha left his job, and for two years he fought 18 hours a day to save the life of a friend he feared would die on a hunger strike undergone for the sake of their shared initiative: they were trying to force Union Carbide to pay, and to make good.

On his website (http://www.indrasinha.com/books/animals-people) Sinha describes his ambition for the novel: he hopes that it 'can make a difference to the Bhopalis and help them in their campaign'. The Bhopal Medical Clinic, which he founded — writing an appeal for funds in the *Guardian* — has helped 30,000 people since 1994 and a percentage of the cover price of *Animal's People* contributes to that appeal. Even as I scrolled through the greetings on his website, his first concern was to make sure I knew how to sign up to the DEC's appeal for the victims of the 2009 war in Gaza, an appeal that the BBC refused to broadcast.

The dramatist Bertolt Brecht is also in this group of politically motivated writers. I do not just have his photograph but also his voice:

sonorous, clear and steady, with its sinister, villainous German accent, recorded by the GDR on the 30 October 1947 when he was asked to attend the House Un-American Activities Committee and answer claims that he was a Communist agitator (the recording is currently in a private collection). The interrogator is pressing him on the translation of a line from a song he had written, *Solidaritätslied*, claiming that the lyric, 'You must be ready to take over' is evidence of a plot to undermine American democracy and install a communist state. The translator of the lyric is called on behalf of the defence and explains that, 'You must be ready to take over' is a wrong translation from the German; a more accurate reading would have been, 'You must be ready to take the lead', and, Brecht insists, it refers not to the takeover of the American political machine, but to the education of the poor. The interrogation drags on for hours. This lyric is torn to pieces. You can hear the stiffness of the tension in the room. Brecht was the only foreigner among a group of successful screenwriters, directors and producers; he was anxious to catch his return flight to Europe the next day.

This group is not for me. The book I am writing now is for children, complete with talking animals, and *Animal Farm* might be described in similar words, but unlike Orwell's novella there is not a political motive in it. This is not to say that children's writers in our time are all without political agendas and motives. Philip Pullman's trilogy, *His Dark Materials*, among other things seeks to deflate Christianity, and the critic Michael Chabon's great love for the work is threatened by the element of Pullman's motive that is in this way political:

> My heart sank as it began to dawn on me, around the time that the first angels begin to show up in *The Subtle Knife*, that there was some devil in Pullman, pitchfork-prodding him into adjusting his story to suit ... the shape of his anti-Church argument (with which I largely sympathize). (Chabon, 2010: 70)

Venturing even further into the realm of politics and children's fiction, Janet Evans, delivered a paper at the University of Exeter that showed startling images from a children's picture book, *The Camp*, which depicted scenes from the holocaust. The author of the book, Oscar K, and the illustrator, Dorte Karrebaek, are politically motivated in the sense that they want to change the way we think about children, and about children's books. Looking forward to the time when he would write *The Camp*, Oscar K said (on his website http://www.oscar-k. dk/text.php), 'If I could depict the holocaust with such gentle grace as Roberto Benigni does in his comedy "Life Is Beautiful," I wouldn't hesitate ... it's not about provoking or offending someone ... books should not necessarily be understood but elicit a desire to understand'.

A similar idea of leading children to understand is discussed by Tess Cosslett in her *Talking Animals In British Children's Fiction, 1786-1914*. She describes in the book how writers such as Thomas Day, Mary Wollstonecraft, Charles Kingsley, and Anna Barbauld and John Aitkin, in their different ways, composed talking-animal stories in order to steer the minds of children towards a sympathetic identification with animals and, thereby, an understanding of God's work — what was understood as Natural Theology.

I love these books and their writers, but I am not among them. I have no wish to change (or form) anyone's mind. I am writing my book about my own children, and how they played their games ... I want to invoke and make use of the part of having children that was delightful, in order to entertain other children. Ask me to talk about such a piece of work in the company of Lara Santoro, George Orwell or Oscar K and the words would snag or die in the air. Their political motive is not in me, gratifying though it would be to claim it.

Writing exercise no. 2: 'Fragments of sensibility'

Imagine you have finished writing your book and that it's published, and in your hands. Imagine opening it and ... imagine the printed text on the page. Write out any old paragraph, a fragment. Carelessly tap into the feeling of it, or tap into a character, or a moment of action — it doesn't matter. Whatever's in your head, concerning your conception of the book — write that. Imagine that you are not composing it, but copying it down from the finished text. Try and identify its effect, the motivation that lies behind it.

The reason I cannot claim it is because a writer's motivation is a component of his or her integrity. We must look at our author photographs, we must check our wardrobes. It is when a writer's character, writing ability and motivation are all three correctly aligned that a forceful literary career is created. We must try and feel the texture of our writing between our fingers, like a tobacco dealer feels the quality of the leaf in the tobacco warehouse, to judge what kind of thing it is — where are its pleasures, what is its burn? And it must be integral to us, not borrowed from writers we admire.

When I think of my own book, *What The Children Saw*, I know it is going to be about someone brought back from the dead; an Easter story. So I have in mind a graveyard, and on either side of the graveyard stand two houses:

> An unearthly quiet hung over both houses — no running feet, no slamming doors — as if the disused church and its graveyard had temporarily reached out on both sides and spread its atmosphere of calm into them ...

I must now rub my own writing between my fingers and find out what it is made of — what is the fuel that is going to enable me to finish it?

2. The sensual motive — the writer as musician

We are in a gloomy corner of Forster's room-of-all-writers. All sorts of drugs are available even if they are vehemently refused; sexual proclivities are of particular interest even if they are to be kept private. Police raids have been known and through the opium smoke we can make out Wilde, Proust, Nicholson Baker, Alan Hollinghurst ... Carol Shields is here. Most of the author photographs show men and women with protuberant, gleaming eyes and soft, un-worked flesh. There is attention to detail in their attire even if it is determinedly plain. There is a tendency for the men to wear feminine clothes and the women to wear masculine ones. For each of these writers, sensual pleasure is their fuel, and they might describe it as a drug. They are concerned particularly with syntax, vocabulary and punctuation. The fall of one word after another is conceived by them with such facility as to inspire in the reader a shiver of nerves. I think of them as writers-as-musicians. Milan Kundera is sometimes here, and writes comprehensively about the relationship between his writing and music in *The Art of the Novel* (1986/2005). These writers are engaged in the stroking of language. They want to seduce. They do not want to explain, exhort, change our ways. The Utopia they seek is a personal, sensual paradise.

As with music, it is in the intelligence of the arrangement as well as in the melody itself that the beauty of the text is to be found. An intelligence that must not only be evident in the sound, the tonality of the text, but also in the delicacy and refinement of its meaning.

The German scholar Sigurd Burckhardt, in an essay titled 'The Poet as Fool and Priest' (1956), supplies an entertaining anecdote, which features a rare glimpse of Goethe as a sculptor, on why writers must orchestrate meaning as a component within the music of the text:

> We know of Goethe that he was prompted to resume work on his 'tragedy of the poet' — *Torquato Tasso* — while he was modelling a foot in a sculptor's studio in Rome. Following this evidently potent impulse, he recast the unfinished play into blank verse and painfully completed it, with what he called 'scarcely justifiable transfusions of my own blood.' What the connection was between modelling and the decision to take up again a long abandoned and extraordinarily difficult project, he did not say; but perhaps one may speculate. While his hands shaped the formless, malleable clay, may he not have wondered about the radical and dismaying difference between the sculptor's medium and his own: between clay-or marble, pigment, tones — and words?
>
> For the difference is radical. All other artists have for their medium what Aristotle called a material cause: more or less shapeless, always meaningless, matter, upon which they can imprint form and meaning. Their media become media proper only under their hands; through shaping they communicate. As artists they are uniquely sovereign, minting unminted bullion into currency, stamping their image upon it. The poet is denied this creative sovereignty. His 'material cause' is a medium before he starts to fashion it; he must deal in an already current and largely defaced coinage. In fact, it is not even a coinage,

but rather a paper currency. Words, as the poet finds them, are tokens for 'real' things, which they are supposed to signify — drafts upon a hoard of reality which it would be too cumbersome to put into circulation. Not merely is the poet denied the privilege of coining his own medium; his medium lacks all corporeality, is a system of signs which have only a secondary, referential substance. (Burckhardt, 1968: 22)

Already I am happier; I am more attuned to this group. My finger moves along the bookshelves and stops at Carol Shields. In *The Stone Diaries* (1993/2008), Shields provides us with a description of a boy called Warren, and she dwells for a moment on his eating habits: 'What he especially loves is to take a slice of boiled ham and fold it over and over in his fingers and then stuff it in his mouth so that the soft sweet meat feels part of his own tongue and inner cheeks' (Shields, 1993/2008: 158). The accuracy in sensation mounts in the music of the text, note by note. Power is given to us in our shared recognition, shared measurement, of this pleasure and we agree with the author, 'That's exactly how it is ... '.

Oscar Wilde took a similar pleasure in creating a gorgeous fall of one word after another, and the sensual achievement, in dramatic terms, of an emotional release. With his frock coats, canes and cravats he dressed as a dandy. In his letters, as well, this compulsion to indulge in the pleasures of the senses can be seen to have been written through his character.

Strangely — so odd! — there is also a glimpse of Orwell in this group: a wistful, ghostly image; impossible to believe it can be true. 'In a peaceful age I might have written ornate or merely descriptive books' (Orwell, 1946/2000: 4).

◆

Alan Hollinghurst was nominated for the Man-Booker prize in 2004 for *The Line of Beauty* (2004). The title comes from a particular double curve, the ogee, an architectural term described by Hogarth as The Line of Beauty. It is also a slang term for cocaine, or it might be the line drawn from the spine around the buttocks; it also refers to the written line. I started to read the novel, and was enchanted. In an article entitled 'The Observer Profile: Alan Hollinghurst', published in the *Observer* (17 October 2004), journalist Geraldine Bedell quotes one of Hollinghurst's close friends, Andrew Motion, as saying about him, 'I can't think of anyone who writes better, line by line'. The 'line by line' part of the judgement was significant, I thought. Hollinghurst won the Newdigate prize for poetry; he cultivates each line for poetic sensibility. It took him six yearss to write the book; for that long he stroked the language to brilliant effect. Like the poet that he is, Hollinghurst writes and rewrites 'at a walking pace' (Geraldine Bedell citing him in the same *Observer* article), a few hundred words per day, worked over and over. His central ambition as a writer is to invoke the musical effect of language. His novels seduce the reader as Andrew Motion said, line by line, and his clever stitching of scenes — which in this novel put love and politics and money and philistinism and madness side by side — result in a series of set-pieces that are rendered with experienced sensuality.

This motivation for the writer, this ambition towards the sensual, is the product of a particular way of thinking. The artistic expression of the novel's meaning is the very point of the subject's existence. 'It is art that makes life, makes interest, makes importance,' wrote Henry James in a letter to H. G. Wells on 10 July 1915, ' ... and I know of no substitute whatever for the force and beauty of its process' (James, 1915/1984: 770).

Hollinghurst signals his debt to Henry James all the way through *The Line Of Beauty*, at one point having his hero, Nick Guest, snort cocaine from the cover of one of James' novels.

In an epigraph to *The Line of Beauty*, Hollinghurst chooses to tease himself concerning the nature of word-by-word, sensual writing. He quotes *Alice in Wonderland*, where the King must choose between two words, 'important — unimportant — unimportant — important'. The King is not guided by their very different meanings. He only wants to find out 'which word sounded best' (Lewis Carroll cited in Hollinghurst, 2004: epigraph).

The story is framed between two general elections, both of which were won by Margaret Thatcher. However, I believe that if a proportion of Hollinghurst's motive was political — to show us the 1980s in all its brutal acquisitiveness — it is a flicker more than a flame. When it appeared, the novel was described as a satire on Thatcherism or a treatise on Thatcherism, and it offers social commentary — 'the wider political context is embraced' (*Daily Star*, 28 January 2005) — but Hollinghurst sticks to his Jamesian strengths: acute observation allied to beautiful expression. He seeks the line of beauty. I do not have any argument with his political insight but I would argue that his 'political embrace' is weak because that is not the fuel this writer is burning, it is not the area in which his talent is generous. Whereas the description of Nick Guest's first kiss with Leo just scoops out the middle of the reader, so sensually, and accurately, is it given to us.

> He felt the coaxing caress of Leo's hand on the back of his head, roaming through the curls there, and then lifted his other hand to stroke Leo's head, so beautifully alien in its hard stubbly angles and the dry dense firmness of his hair. He thought he saw the point of kissing but also its limitations — it was an instinct, a means of expression, of mouthing a passion but not of satisfying it. So his right hand, that was lightly clutching Leo's waist, set off, still doubting its freedom, to dawdle over his plump buttocks and then squeeze them. (Hollinghurst, 2004: 38)

Among this group of sensual writers, some clothes from my own wardrobe can be paraded: the frock coat, in mink grey, made out of a fabric that contains a proportion of aluminium so that it remains looking crushed; the fitted pin-striped jeans that satirize the shapeless pin-striped suit trouser; the expensive Italian boots in distressed leather with laces wrapped round the body of the foot to make them look like something Byron has worn and discarded. Here, in this group, these garments are welcomed. My taste for whisky is understood. The pleasures of the flesh are alive in the eyes of all around me.

When I wake up I have a hangover, but I know that I have found the fuel I wish to burn, to use up, in writing *What The Children Saw*. It will be gorgeous.

I realize I have not brought with me any method of gathering and transporting fuel, so now, during the first rewriting of this text, I remember the green plastic fuel container I use to fill the lawnmower; and I summon it, and carry it away with me, brimful.

I can tap into this surge of energy, given to me by these other writers that I find myself among, and I can carry on. Where was I, with that earlier fragment? A resurrection story, an Easter story. I had two houses standing on either side of a graveyard, and perhaps I will now summon the church itself, in the middle of the graveyard.

> Imagine, if you will, a church so long abandoned that the leaves blown into its porch pile up against the door in heaps that shift from one side to another depending on the strength and direction of the wind, and are never disturbed by human footfall, or by human hand turning the iron key in the lock and pulling the handle, but instead are only unsettled by mice and spiders and by that indifferent wind, again, that brought last year's leaves, and the year's before that, for as long as anyone might remember ...

3. The existential motive

I am still trying –- difficult with a thumping headache — to screw on the wretchedly badly made fuel cap before any more precious drops spill, when I notice a more anxious and morbid group of writers in Forster's room. These writers station themselves apart from everyone else and stare too hard, for too long. They are restless, prone to febrile introspection but they are shot through with dark veins of humour. They are Godless.

They will tame the beast of absurdity; that is the fuel that drives them. Kafka, Kundera again, Sartre with his side-parting, round spectacles and brushed back hair, and that stare. Simone de Beauvoir, with her centre-parting but the same stare, is here with him.

The story of God was dismantled by Darwin; the sky overhead is no longer heaven but a limitless dark. They ask us to look into it, and when that commonplace vertigo has us in its grip, they wish for all of us to step over the edge and experience with them the terrifying freedom of the fall into the abyss.

In Kafka's *The Trial* (1925), Joseph K is arrested and charged for a crime of which he has no knowledge. He is released without reason, fights against an incomprehensible bureaucracy to clear his name, and is then executed for no reason. Kafka's story, like Orwell's *Animal Farm*, is an allegory, yet Kafka was driven by different motives. Orwell's farm animals warn us against the perils of communist revolution, whereas K's fight is apparently against a complex, inexplicable legal system, which is a hard-working metaphor for our struggle to find life's meaning.

Milan Kundera, a committed sponsor of Kafka (the K's all colliding in their surnames in a comical sort of Amis-esque tumble), sums it up in *The Art of the Novel* (1986) when he says that in *The Trial* ' ... we see all the anxiety, ambiguity, and hope of our spiritual life projected into the very concrete realities of a judicial system and bureaucracy. *The Trial* reads as absurd to the extent that it discusses the spiritual life in terms of concrete, everyday realities' (Kundera, 1986/2005: 73).

Albert Camus, also loitering critically but even further estranged from the general goings-on, suggested that Kafka did not go far enough — his works contained a glimmer of hope. Camus proposed that life was akin to the fate of Sisyphus, the mythical figure required to roll a boulder up to the top of the mountain, only to have it roll back down, over and over again.

And Tennyson appears suddenly: 'So runs my dream: but what am I? /An infant crying in the night: /An infant crying for the light: /And with no language but a cry' (Tennyson, 1850/2008: Canto 54, ln.18–20).

I veer away. I was interested, once, but I am no longer inclined to foster or explore despair; it is so easily and plentifully available in real life that I wish any story I am going to write (especially this one, since it is for, or maybe just about, children) to go in the opposite direction; it should secrete optimism and wonder, and yes, sensual pleasure.

This group is not for me. I have much-loved copies of these works on my shelves but they are dusty and flyblown, long untouched. There is something blinding, terrifying, about them. A monster depression looms. My finger passes over them, but nonetheless I am still looking; and my finger points further along the shelves, until I stumble into a landscape.

4. The artist motive — the writer as painter

Here is a group — V. S. Naipaul, James Joyce, Ian McEwan, Kevin Barry — which gives me an immediate sense of excitement. It leads me to think, after only moments in their company, that I must have this type of fuel, and another type of engine to burn it, so I can tap into this motive as well.

They are writers-as-painters; they must capture, in a distinctive way, the truth of what they see in front of their eyes. They wear sensible, good-quality clothes for the work that faces them.

In his short story 'Atlantic City' (2007), Kevin Barry's subject is the looks, the gait, the stance, the top-to-bottom character of the pool-playing youth, James. How cleverly he gives us a sketch of his physical appearance and his gait: 'the width of a small van across the shoulders, and he moved noiselessly, as though on castors' (Barry, 2007: 2), before he draws away to allow us a breathing space and to see Broad Street as it 'revelled in the languor of evening heat' (Barry, 2007: 3), returning to give us more brushwork on James's character. In this way he allows each layer of paint to dry before he adds the next, and each time a layer is added, it changes — deepens — our perception of the character. The seemingly rock-solid confidence of this youth, and the sympathy Barry has carefully elicited for him, with his kindness to the younger children, his grace and skill at the pool table and at the pinball machine, and most importantly his sense of humour, is subtly questioned by his crude over-confidence with the girls. Between each layer of colour, Kevin Barry takes us outside again, to refresh our view. And then comes a stand-out line from the local policeman, Garda Ryan, as the latter squares up to James' cheek, 'I don't care whose family you're from' (Barry, 2007: 11). With this line Kevin Barry allows us a final insight, the submerged part of James's character is not confident at all, but instead the opposite: James is trying to live up to his family's reputation. He is like the cartoon character having run off the edge of the cliff: running fast, but with nothing except thin air below. The picture is complete. This allows Barry, when he abruptly spins us forward ten years, to show us James's fate: 'on a low September evening [James] would swim out too far and drown' (Barry, 2007: 12). In just half an hour's reading, Barry produces a perfectly realized portrait.

These writers are painters of landscape, both geographical and psychological. They are skilled purveyors of the truth evident in places and in people: V. S. Naipaul's extravagant understanding of his misplaced cast of characters in the assembly of short stories, *In A Free State* (1971); Somerset Maugham's obsessive sketching of people and places in his commonplace book, *A Writer's Notebook* (1949); Joyce's painterly eye in *Dubliners* (1914).

Ian McEwan is here too. *Atonement* opens with a portrait of a child's frustrated attempt at recruiting her reluctant cousins to take part in a display of amateur dramatics. This mood of lingering crossness is augmented by her witnessing the sexual congress between adults (enough to make anyone, child or not, resentful) and her bad mood becomes so great that it leads to her final act of betrayal-by-silence. It is a heartbreaking, poignant study of a pre-pubescent girl; and it is built with scrupulous logic.

Marcel Proust, meanwhile, has sauntered over here from the sensualists' group (always taking one path or another, always hither and thither) and Forster himself, this room's host, sums it up,

> ... how amazingly does Proust not only describe French Society, not only the working of his characters, but the personal equipment of the reader, so that one keeps stopping with a gasp to say 'Oh, how did he find that out about me? I didn't even know it about myself until he informed me, but it is so'. (Forster, 1925: 11)

I have a fuel can in each hand now and it leads me to think of writers who use this combination of fuels. Just as Hollinghurst declared his motivation in the epigraph to *The Line of Beauty*, Carol Shields exactly defines her motivation as a mixture of the musician and the artist, when she chooses Judith Downing's poem, 'The Grandmother Cycle', as an epigraph for *The Stone Diaries*. The poem describes how

---

Writing exercise no. 3: 'Points of colour'

First of all, before starting this exercise, read *Camera Lucida* by Roland Barthes, and *Poetry in the Making* by Ted Hughes. Use your powers of observation to paint the ordinary scene that you first imagined in your 'wurge' — the first writing exercise in this book. Concentrate on accuracy, and the correct choice of distinctive details.

Shields will deliver this faux-biography first as a painter, ' ... but still her life / could be called a monument //shaped in a slant /of available light', and then as a musician, ' ... and set to the movement /of possible music' (Shields, 1993/2008: epigraph).

So, I will carry both these fuel cans — writing as a painter and as a musician — and even while I welcome the sense of balance (carrying objects of equal weight, one in each hand), it strikes me there might be a third group ... and it is thinking about what happened to my motor car that leads me to realize it is true, and it is a big omission, perhaps because there is just a whiff of shame to it.

5. The entertainment motive

Last year I was driving home when the note made by the car's engine dived, tailed off, stuttered and then died. I prodded the accelerator to no effect. It was a brand new, expensive car; surely it could not break down.

Powerless, we coasted to a halt, blocking the single track lane. The children disappeared in a trice, walking — no, running — home. The AA swiftly came and plugged a computer into the dash and noted down the fault codes from the internal computer.

I had put petrol in a diesel engine. They towed it to the garage and provided a hire car immediately.

How quickly and completely the journey had come to an end, because I had put in the wrong fuel. The car was a useless lump of metal and I was left stranded. It was embarrassing to have caused this obstruction in the lane.

I had messed up my grand new vehicle, and the fact that it was grand and new is perhaps relevant because some among this group of writers (so many of them; it is crowded here) are the wealthiest of all. Their ambition is to entertain: Arthur Conan Doyle, Agatha Christie, Georges Simenon, Hergé (if I am allowed sort-of-graphic novels), John Mortimer. They are low, middle and high brow. Among them are Edgar Allan Poe, Charles Dickens, Jane Austen, Graham Greene, Deborah Moggach. I love them for their sanity and for the gracefulness of their expression. Jane Austen writes in her velvety voice, during this extraordinary, mocking dance she performs with other romantic novelists in the opening chapters of *Northanger Abbey* (1818), and describes perfectly the writing we all wish to undertake and produce, ' … some work in which the greatest powers of the mind are displayed, in which the most thorough knowledge of human nature, the happiest delineation of its varieties, the liveliest effusions of wit and humour are conveyed to the world in the best chosen language' (Austen, 1818/1934: 33)

Early in his career, Graham Greene defined some of his novels (e.g *The Ministry of Fear* [1943]) as 'entertainments' so as to cast them in a different light from the so-called literary works that he thought more highbrow. And yet, as his career matured, the distinction became blurred and perhaps the happiest result was the film and the novella of *The Third Man* (1949).

Either increasingly beloved or forgotten after they are dead, members of this group are liable to be looked down on by their contemporaries, particularly if they are inordinately successful. Evelyn Waugh, in the Catholic magazine, *Commonweal,* said of Graham Greene that his was 'not a specifically literary style at all. The words are functional, devoid of sensuous attraction, of ancestry, and of independent life' (Waugh, 1948: 323). Daphne du Maurier was similar in being critically frowned on during her life but her reputation is being lifted, bit by bit, not least because The University of Exeter has championed her work (it holds the du Maurier archive).

I am with Michael Chabon: we must elevate this instinct — to entertain — to its rightful place: as high as you please. He makes a powerful plea to those who underrate it.

But maybe these intelligent and serious people, my faithful straw men, are wrong. Maybe the reason for the junkiness of so much of what pretends to entertain us is that we have accepted — indeed we have helped to articulate — such a narrow, debased concept of entertainment. The brain is an organ of entertainment, sensitive at any depth, and over a wide spectrum. But we have learned to mistrust and despise our human aptitude for being entertained, and in that sense we get the entertainment we deserve.

I'd like to believe that, because I read for entertainment, and I write to entertain. Period. Oh, I could decoct a brew of other, more impressive motivations and explanations. I could uncork some stuff about reader response theory, or the Lacanian *parole*. I could go on about the storytelling impulse and the need to make sense of experience through story. A spritz of Jung might scent the air. I could adduce Kafka's formula: 'A book must be an ice-axe to break the seas frozen inside our soul.' I could go down to the cafe at the local mega-bookstore and take some wise words of Abelard or Koestler about the power of literature off a mug. But in the end — here's my point — it would still all boil down to *entertainment*, and its suave henchman, pleasure. Because when the axe bites the ice, you feel an answering throb of delight all the way from your hands to your shoulders, and the blade rolls like a bell for miles. (Chabon, 2010: 1)

The motive of these writers is to entertain and delight readers. If this motive transfers (and it usually does) to an instinct to entertain a multitude, it will necessarily require becoming good at plot, writing at the dramatic end of the spectrum (in many ways the deep end) where hungers a broad audience, highbrow and low. The result (perhaps not directly sought or expected, but also, perhaps, a central motivation) is that they become popular and rich. And because they will be developing the story-skills of a dramatist, their work is more likely to be adapted for the screen.

If we have described writers as painters and as musicians already, we are actorly, in this group, in that we crave the sound of applause in our ears, and we can regard this in ourselves as either a cry for attention or a generous instinct to give pleasure; both are true. I say 'we' because I am so much a part of this group that I hardly know it. Am I allowed a third source of fuel? The sides of my analogy are creaking;

there is no hybrid car with three types of motor. But we do not like to be pigeon-holed, to be pushed here and there and assigned to categories, and given labels.

I have spent long enough in Forster's room, talking about different types of fuel. There is only so much beating that any analogy can take before the life goes out of it. Analogies, after a while, are like the sea-trout that can be found every November caught by the gills in the iron grate in the leat outside my house. They are spent-out. The females have dropped their eggs, the males have fertilized them, and neither has any energy left. Having fought their way upstream to the point of exhaustion — to the exact pool where they themselves hatched — now they allow themselves to be carried downstream, battered and injured, and a proportion of them are diverted into this ancient, hand-dug mining waterway. I hoick them out and knock them on the head to shorten their suffering, and I put them on the fence posts so I can watch the buzzards — or crows — pulling at their remains.

However, for the sake of being complete, I must slip the trout back into the river and ask them to hold position for a while longer, because I need to include two more groups of writers. Both groups focus on what is wrong with the world, and the stance of both groups is curative, medicinal. However, there the comparison ends and they could not be more dissimilar.

6. The therapeutic motive

The first of these two groups — a large one, especially among early-career novelists — contains those who write as a therapeutic process: to mend themselves.

By the time Virginia Woolf was fifteen, and within a period of two years, her mother had committed suicide and her half-sister had died. The family doctor issued a prescription to help her cope with her first mental breakdown. Part of that prescription was that she should write a diary.

To write out a problem, to describe unhappiness, is a mode of confession and it mends in a similar way; like a prayer, it is a call to an invisible power — and to one's fellow man — to understand, and such an understanding is its cure, given time.

Virginia Stephen should have married someone else. As soon as she married Leonard Woolf, she was lumbered with a toxic name. Just to hear it makes one feel unhappy, with that call of sexual repression from the forename; and one instinctively recoils from the sharp-toothed danger of the surname in which one hears the wolf's bark, at the same time as catching sight of it, and then one must consider oneself being eaten whole, wolfed down. 'A dreadful weariness came over me, that we should still be the same people, in the same bodies; wandering not quite alive, not yet suffered to die, in a pale light' (Woolf, 2004: ix).

I feel the same impatience as if someone were ill: it is their lot, even if it is not their fault, and they must get over it, and please do not pass it on to *me*.

Doris Lessing wrote out her own breakdown in the differently coloured notebooks that interleave the Free Women sections in *The Golden Notebook*. Dickens meanwhile used the process of writing to find out what was wrong with his marriage, as Jane Smiley describes:

> All through the writing of *David Copperfield*, he loved David and the other characters and identified strongly with them. He was especially sorry to see them go when the novel was completed. More important, he was convinced at the end of David's story that his own story could and should turn out differently than it had in real life. He wrote to his friend John Forster that he longed for the companionship of a woman such as David's Agnes rather than that of his own wife, Catherine. Shortly after the publication of David Copperfield, he began to entertain ideas of linking up with other women — first his earliest love, who happened to send him a letter, but turned out, upon meeting, to be a disappointment, and later Ellen Ternan, whom he met in a dramatic performance of a play he had written with Wilkie Collins, and who became his friend and mistress for thirteen years. In the absence of trained professional help, Dickens became his own psychoanalyst, exploring his childhood youth, diagnosing his circumstances and needs ... through writing his novel, he did observe himself and then act upon his observations, which is the paradigm of the therapeutic act. (Smiley, 2006: 40)

If this is our motivation we must take it seriously: there is a duty, in confession and in self-healing, to do something extraordinary to oneself, and scoop from the very bottom of the barrel, see into every hidden corner of our own minds.

Writing exercise no. 4: 'Confession'

If it's the case that you're writing partly in order to mend yourself, you will know immediately the core of your hurt, and its cause. Write another 'wurge' — as in the first exercise — but think of nothing but the confessional. You are seated not at the table, but at the confessional. The white of the paper is where the confession will take place. No one will read it; it is private. Only later will you attempt to turn this confession into a story for someone else to read. For now, simply write, without stopping, for two minutes. Perhaps even do this every day, for a while. Scoop out the bottom of that core of hurt or disappointment, and for now keep it close to yourself. In a few days' time you will read it again.

---

7. The comedic motive

To segue from self-therapy to comedy I want to summon the image of Kafka again, but this time as a vision of the writer unable to stop laughing all the way through his reading out loud of *The Metamorphosis* (1915) to his friend Max Brod.

The poet, novelist and composer of short stories Gerard Woodward also had a foot in both camps (therapeutic and comedic) while writing *I'll Go to Bed at Noon* (2004), bringing a dark humour to his family's wrestle with the wretched booze.

Perhaps comedy is the perfect self-therapy; certainly it is not a huge step to go from the self-therapists to this most glorious, down-in-the-dirt and magical of all groups of writers, whose burning desire is common as muck and heaven-sent, and more difficult than all the others put together, and at the same time, given the instinct, as easy as slipping on a banana skin: to make us laugh. Barbara Pym, J. P. Donleavy, Stella Gibbons, Michael Frayn, they are all here, but there is perhaps no greater example in English letters of the comedic motive being written into the character of a writer than that of P. G. Wodehouse.

If I steer away from the existentialists and the self-therapists, I wholeheartedly want to join this group of comic writers. Do I look like them, am I one of them? I did not have any idea of how Wodehouse looked, or how he dressed. I expected plus-fours and a weak chin, like Bertie Wooster. Instead, scrolling through Google Images, I found a sleek, brillianteened man more like Noël Coward. Nonetheless we can summon him.

I once had cause to look through a P. G. Wodehouse archive that was kept in the attic of a private house and I came across a story about his life that I have subsequently learned is common knowledge, but I knew nothing of it at the time. It is a fable that warns what might happen if you try and run a petrol engine on diesel fuel.

In the summer of 1940, just as the war was turning from phoney to serious, Wodehouse was living near Le Touquet in France. One morning he wandered out of his villa to find German soldiers on the lawn. England's premier comic novelist was then driven to an internment camp in Belgium and processed. Shortly afterwards he was returned to his villa and placed under house arrest.

Herr Plack, Goebbel's assistant, saw that by chance he had, in a gentle kind of captivity, a man in a unique way emblematic of England, and a man who, it seemed, was not averse to having German officers — if they were in the neighbourhood — drop in for a bath or attend a party. Plack lifted Wodehouse out of Belgium and gave him a comfortable room in the Adlon hotel in Berlin. He himself spoke English fluently, and no doubt there were sessions in the hotel bar exchanging jokes about golf, and marriage, and elderly relatives. Plack saw immediately that he was dealing with someone of great political value, but without political sense — a man who could only try and be funny. He invited Wodehouse to broadcast over German radio to Britain.

There was no heavy-handed censorship; Plack knew that it could only work in his favour to let his subject loose. And so, from Berlin, there came into British homes a stream of affectionate, funny broadcasts by P. G. Wodehouse. Some were about life in an internment camp: 'The chief trouble is that it means you are away from home for a long time. When I join my wife I'd better take along a letter of introduction, just to be on the safe side'. Others were about the Germans: 'Just as I'm about to feel belligerent about some country I meet a decent sort of chap. We go out together and lose any fighting thoughts or feelings'. Or they were about the war: 'The only concession I want from Germany is that she gives me a loaf of bread, tells the gentlemen with the muskets at the main gate to look the other way, and leaves the rest to me. In return I am prepared to hand over India, an autographed set of my books, and to reveal the secret process of cooking sliced potatoes on a radiator'.

In Britain he had been loved; suddenly his books were taken off library shelves, the BBC banned his song lyrics from being aired, he was accused of being a quisling and in Parliament it was suggested that if he ever dared to return to this country he must be charged with treason, for which the maximum punishment was execution.

With a proper sense of natural justice, of brotherhood between two writers who, in different ways, were victims of the strength of their motivation, Wodehouse was rescued by the foremost political writer of the age, the man who cared most about fairness, and justice, and political morality — George Orwell. In 1945, just as the war in Europe was coming to a close and it could be expected that Wodehouse might wish to return to England, Orwell composed a long and detailed defence of Wodehouse's character and his behaviour.

Wodehouse's only concern had been to quicken someone's smile, and enjoy his own humour. He could be accused of being stupid, and of being thoughtless, but he was neither a fascist, nor a traitor. He was a comic ingénue just like so many of his characters. When Plack poured politics into him, it could only find its way out as humour. Orwell said in his conclusion, ' … if we drive him to retire to the United States and renounce his British citizenship we shall end by being horribly ashamed of ourselves'.[1]

This first analogy, the burn, is now done with. I do not say that each book by any particular author might not have a different fuel from his or her last one. I do not say that you cannot use more than one fuel in the same book. After all, as I finally press a new cartridge into my

Lamy pen and prepare to make notes towards the writing of *What The Children Saw*, I am proposing to use three different types — as entertainer, musician and painter — in more or less equal proportions. And of course underlying all the motives previously mentioned are these bread-and-butter motives of all writers that I mentioned earlier: that of personal glory — even in obscurity — and, of course, money, and the prosecution of an individual world view or *theory*.

What is important to know is which fuels are most suited to us for the work in hand in the same way that our clothes must be suited to us. Recently I am becoming more interested in looking at what clothes writers wear, what is the type of gleam in their eye, how they stand — because as I have said before (but it bears repeating), when the novelist's clothes, and her character, her life, her motivation and her aptitude for writing in a particular way all run together in the same direction, then he or she is imbued with integrity and the writing is its effective outpouring. Clothes are a signifier of motivation. Where would T. E. Lawrence be without his costume?

Ivy Compton-Burnett used to hide her handkerchiefs in her 'breeks' — her knickers — which was a perfectly odd and funny habit, in tune with her output. Oscar Wilde was at the forefront of a movement that wished to reform dress. Evelyn Waugh insisted that his London tailor make him a suit out of cloth that was intended only for making working men's flat caps. Dr Vike Plock, in an article shortly to be published in the journal *Modernism/modernity*, points out the link between Elizabeth Bowen's writing and her dress sense and finds an expression of it, straight from the author's mouth:

> In her essays Bowen consistently returns to this assertion that fashion and subjectivity are intimately linked. 'Clothes ... never remain a question of pure æsthetics; far too much personal feeling is involved in them.' Were it not for this intriguing connection between dress and psychology, garments, robes, and other millinery objects would not be such complex and intricate texts waiting to be deciphered.

We must be comfortable both in our skins and in the work — and thus we have found our footing. A boxing trainer will tell his man that the power in his punch comes not from his fist but from the floor that he pushes against, with his feet. And if, in the same way, we have an alignment of character, motivation and writing skill, the energy will be used to good effect — we can more accurately deliver to the reader the necessary heat, we can make the burn.

Postscript

When I mentioned to a colleague that I was writing this analogy he quietly announced that he thought it was a bad idea. 'To suggest to anyone who wants to write a novel, and particularly to a young person, that they should light a fire inside themselves ... ' (he has this kindly way of denouncing what he thinks is poor work) ' ... well, I can hardly think of worse advice,' he said, mildly.

My analogy lay in ruins. There are few people more experienced and capable in the propagation of good writing as this man and his objection was as follows: writing fiction is a narcissistic business and any hope of success must lie in the writer's learning to douse the flames of egoism that rear up and engulf the *morsel* of objective intelligence thats is left inside *anyone* once the notion of 'being a writer' is entertained. It is *outside* him or herself that a writer must look, for there to be any hope of success. He dreaded the prospect of having to read any results of the influence my analogy might have on his students. Stop now, he advised me.

I was chastened, but in the way of these things, late at night, staring at a ceiling made into a grey, distant fuzz by hours of darkness, my own egotism reared up, and announced an idea that might answer my colleague's concerns and at the same time allow me to stick with my analogy.

At the earliest opportunity I put it to him. He was hurrying around the quad, fighting with all the swing doors, which were locked. 'What if I add a postcript,' I said when I caught up with him. 'It's the *control* of the burn that is of critical importance in this respect,' I went on. 'In a petrol engine the correct mix of fuel and air is regulated by the carburettor; in a gas kiln the fineness of the nozzles through which the fuel is injected must be adjusted correctly.' I could see he was reverting to his earlier dismay. 'To light a barbecue is easy,' I continued, 'but it's essential to wait until the first, vigorous burning has been spent otherwise the food will be charred on the outside and raw on the inside. And a spray gun filled with water should be kept to hand because the fat from the meat will drip onto the hot charcoal and catch fire, and flames will leap up ... The water is sprayed on to damp them down.'

This element of control would be an essential postscript to the analogy, I proposed. Did I have his blessing to continue? He saw he had lost me to the same overwrought enthusiasm that he has spent a lifetime battling against in his students. I must repeat therefore: any burner of fuel should have its control mechanisms functioning properly if it is to work, from the vents on a wood stove, to the length of the wick on a candle, or the amount of suck on a pipe stem — and so it must be with writing.

For 'control mechanism' read self-criticism allied with technique — both subjects which I will return to later on — and the combination to some extent determines writing style. It is like a mathematical equation:

$$\text{Motivation} + \text{technique} + \text{voice} = \text{style}$$

One could cite as a control mechanism for Orwell a prose style that was forged during a career in journalism. Accuracy, simplicity and clarity of expression were its prescribed qualities, the same as those required of a good witness in a court of law. Orwell refused to use combinations of words that already sounded familiar together, so that each sentence should strike the ear as freshly made, and carrying its meaning succinctly. These were skills that he combined with narrative invention, in *Animal Farm* and in *Nineteen Eighty-Four*, to produce the simple authority that makes so credible his invented worlds. He refused to let the material run away with him; he realized that if the story was fantastic, then the language had to be deeply plain. He curtailed the excitement of the writing, he turned that particular dial anticlockwise; consequently these extraordinary creations were delivered in a deadpan, flat tone that brought them to life more vigorously than any Wildean flourish could ever have done. They are a pair of grotesque, world-changing novels. They smell of gunpowder and smoke.

The control mechanisms used by Brecht were as newly minted as communism itself. He took the principles proposed by the Russian formalist Shklovsky, the notion of 'ostranenie', of art's 'making strange' by virtue of its fabric and surface, and adapted it into his famous 'estrangement' creating an objectifying distance between the drama and its audience. Brecht believed that story-telling had been a corrupting influence because, due to its power to enchant the human mind, it had created false belief (i.e. *The Bible*, various authors), and he constructed his dramatic narratives in order to disengage this facility, to puncture the enchantment, by informing the audience from the outset that they were not allowed to be seduced by the experience of the drama. They could enjoy it, but, like with a Richard Rogers building, they were to be told how it was built, to be shown behind the scenes as it were, and to stand at a proper, grown-up distance. In this way they were invited to consider the intellectual arguments, judgements and so on, that its author laid in front of them. He achieved his purpose with a robust delicacy.

Oscar Wilde's control mechanism was to have the good taste — good manners, essentially — to overstep the mark by just the right amount and inject sufficient humour and refresh our wisdom, in order to take us with him, and to use the contrivances of plot in the same way, to keep us on his side.

I have a potential opening paragraph for *What The Children Saw* and now I will summon the characters; they have work to do. I will use a paintbrush to make accurate portraits of them, I will listen out for the music of the text. I will approach the start of the drama — an adventure story that I hope will capture every man, woman or child, whether of elite sensibility or not, who reads it. This first piece of writing will be a test, just to write myself into the next part of the process. So I might write indulgently, go on for a bit too long, and probably none of it will be used. But I will cast an eye, see what I have got — who I have got.

I already have the church, long abandoned, and the leaves in its porch moving from one corner to another. Now I will take a couple of pages in order to see the graveyard that surrounds it, and to find the children themselves in their houses on either side:

> The graveyard spread itself around the church's skirts to the extent of three acres. It was overgrown, tangled with creepers and filled with broken crosses, tombstones that had sunk and tilted half over and crypts that yawned open; these things frightened some of the people who ventured here, but there were four children for whom it was their playground. They'd lived for all their lives on either side of it: one girl, Megan, aged 9, on Buller Road which ran along the western edge, and three siblings, Emma, David and Ben, aged 9, 7 and 6 years, on Kitchener Lane, a higgledy-piggledy road which marked its eastern boundary.
>
> Megan was an only child. It was she who would phone the others to suggest doing things; they had the careless luxury of each other's company whereas Megan wandered alone in her house, below the glass ceiling that stopped her looking up to the adult world, and her strangely green eyes (the colour of Smarties), and her thoughts, almost the direction in which she habitually stood, were fixed on their house. When they answered the phone her first words were always the same, 'Is Emma there?' spoken in such an odd, blank voice as if she didn't know the person who'd answered, had never visited them, whereas the truth was she spent more time in their bedrooms, in their kitchen, in their living rooms, than in her own. When she did get

---

Writing exercise no. 5: 'Celebrations'

Write down the story of a regular social event that you enjoy, but then write it again while consciously adopting a different motivation. Everything will change: the choice of observations, the syntax, the rhythm, the whole tilt of the piece.

Feel which ones are right for you. Sometimes you will delude yourself. For instance, we might delude ourselves that a piece of writing is funny. To generalize unfairly, if you are sunny and personable in real life you are unlikely to be a naturally comic writer. If you are hurt and taciturn and hateful and angry and socially inept, then it is more likely.

We can make a start on our novel because we have a source of energy, a motive for bothering to write, that will see us through the difficulties of its manufacture.

---

herself in their company she could be a touch bossy; even her brown hair bobbed in a confident way and she had the stance of that kind of girl — knees locked straight, feet slightly apart, hips thrust forward — but all this was because she wished, always so, so wished, to have the others near her, and not only that, but she wished for them to be pleased to be near her. If she could achieve this often enough it made up for not having brothers and sisters of her own.

The others, meanwhile, rampaged through their house with or without Megan and wore it out three times as quickly: the washing machine whirled all day; the crockery broke, one item after another; the soap, the food, the pens and pencils — all the resources of the house — disappeared in a trice. Emma, with the custard-yellow hair which was long enough so that if she tilted her head she could make it hang in a curtain away from her face, was always in the fridge or banging the food cupboards or stepping in and out of the shower, the glass door squeaking on a weakening hinge. She was the same age as Megan and she was good all the way through like a stick of rock with the word Emma written in it; she was beloved and loving and she cared deeply about being good and honourable almost despite herself, especially when she was led astray by her liking for chocolate and cake and biscuits. David used up electricity more than anything, having a 100 watt lamp over his model table and two computers in use or on stand-by, plus the phone and various toys' battery-packs charging. He looked frail as a leaf with blue eyes large as saucers but he was never hurt, ill or injured, and he was clever, but found it impossible to tell the truth about circumstances which might place him in a poor light. Ben was the youngest and funniest, and mostly used up people's patience. He made the most of every word by saying it loudly and would as often as possible try to raise a laugh, but when he tried too hard he became irritating.

Together these four children had grown used to the graveyard's sights and sounds. The soul of the place, its quietude, its long silences, the inscriptions dedicated to those dead and forgotten, its creaturely inhabitants (the foxes, stoats, butterflies, weasels, rabbits, mice, badgers, beetles and worms), its dark, mossy places that embraced them and its stinging nettle patches that repelled them, and not forgetting the shadowy recesses under the monkey-puzzle tree — all this, taken together, was their spiritual home and the familiar setting for their long and involved games.

I am finding my way towards the beginning, writing my way through the page, but now I have to stop and think — because I am an entertainer — about how I am going to engineer *story* right from the outset.

Note

1. The quotes I have used are taken from Orwell's essay, 'In Defence of PG Wodehouse' (1945/2000).

2. The Alchemist

The chronology of the industrial process (the writing of this novel) demands we move to the next step and perform its manufacture. From our previous analogy, The Burn, we carry with us a motivating force, that alchemists would have called 'the vulgar fire' and they offered the figure of Vulcan as representative of that element.

The alchemist Francis Bacon stands Vulcan next to another important figure, Daedalus. 'Vulcan or Daedalus (that is, the furnace or engine)' (Bacon, 1905: 423). Daedalus means 'cunning worker' and if Vulcan is the burn, then Daedalus is the engine. This is our urgent wish now, to get on and make. This impatience, the desire to rush into print, is a feature of the novelist's character, generally speaking and especially the apprentice novelist.

E. E. Cummings advises us that writers are people 'who are obsessed by Making' (Herbert and Hollis, 2000: 53), and the analogy I will invoke in order to explore the manufacture of fiction is that of the writer-as-alchemist.

I first followed this train of thought — the writer-as-alchemist — when the critic Fiammetta Rocco wrote a review of my novel, *The Unnumbered* (2004) in *The Economist* (29 April 2004). It contained a phrase that naturally I seized on; she suggested the novel ' ... should be read by anyone who believes in the transforming power of fiction.'

It became one of those phrases that cropped up everywhere. I could not listen to a literary commentary without hearing it expounded. But what did she mean — what was this 'transforming power' of fiction? I understood it to be a transformation of the reader — at the very least a temporary, sensual transformation. The reader would approach the fiction in one state, would read the work, and be transformed by its processes into another state.

The question was: transformed from what, to what? From a lower to a higher position, I was sure: from relative ignorance to knowledge and truth, from confusion and cloudiness to understanding and clarity. The reader would be walked forward a pace or two in the dawdle that is one's growing, progressive conception of what life is and what it should be. And to wreak this kind of effect on a reader is the ambition of writers, so that a novel of theirs might become a milestone in the reader's consciousness, part of the fabric of its expansion.

But how was a novel supposed to do this? It is clear that a factual text can do the same thing: to read a particular history, for instance Misha Glenny's description of the globalization of crime, *McMafia* (2008/2009), or to read a book about the feathered edges of the human brain's behaviour, such as Oliver Sacks' *The Man Who Mistook His Wife for a Hat* (1985/2007), is to have one's perception transformed.

The writer of fiction aims to achieve the same ascension of the reader, but by virtue of making it up, by inventing. Therefore, an additional kind of transformation is required: the ingredients of life (i.e. reality) must first be assembled and thereafter manipulated before they can be transformed into fiction. In order to create in readers, in their turn, a transformative epiphany.

There is something of the magician, the alchemist, in the person who can perform this 'pleasant and sportive fiction of the transformation of bodies' (Bacon, 1905: 822), who can manipulate the base materials of life, apply pressure to them, until they are transformed and given extraordinary value.

Why alchemists, and not chemists? Alchemy, after all, is an outmoded science; it was the precursor of chemistry; the adepts at alchemy lacked knowledge and resorted to bluster and pretence and magic and lying. Raymond Lully, a relatively recent adept, was apparently hired by Edward II and shown to a workbench in the Tower of London where he transmuted from base metal 50,000 pounds worth of gold coins ,which were used to help finance the Crusades. Afterwards he went on to live to the age of one hundred and fifty, all the while able to run and jump like a youth.

There was no limit to the ambition, the bluster and the myth-making. The alchemist Artephius, in his *The Art of Prolonging Human Life* (circa 1200), claimed that he had ' ... now lived one thousand years or thereabouts' (www.alchemylab.com, 2010).

Alchemy liked to pretend that it was chemistry. Surely, in the modern day, the writer-as-chemist would be more consistently successful, more accurate, more true, than the writer-as-alchemist?

Johann Wolfgang von Goethe was successful both as a scientist and as a writer. He wrote a novel, *Elective Affinities* (1809), which proposed that chemistry underpinned human psychological behaviour. The novel's opening thesis is that we react with one another like chemicals, either attracting each other (in the case of people who do have an affinity), or repelling one another (in the case of those who do not). Meanwhile the insertion of character C to the mix of characters A and B might cause A and B to split asunder, and A and C to join together causing B to be ejected on its own.

This is the fate of Charlotte (in Goethe's novel) when she and her husband, Eduard, invite the Captain to stay on their estate for an extended period. Immediately on his arrival the Captain forms an energetic friendship with Eduard and Charlotte is left to her own devices. All three happily compare themselves to chemical substances and reactions. 'What we call limestone,' says the Captain, 'is a more or less pure oxide of calcium tightly combined with a weak acid known to us in gaseous form. If a piece of that rock is placed in dilute sulphuric acid this combines with the calcium to form gypsum; the gaseous weak acid, on the other hand, escapes' (Goethe, 1809/1994: 33).

Charlotte objects to being 'that poor creature' (Goethe, 1809/1994: 33), the gaseous vapour which escapes and is left on its own. As she points out, it 'may have a great deal to put up with' (Goethe, 1809/1994: 33).

It is proposed that a fourth character is added to the mixture, so that Charlotte will not be lonely. Together they decide on Ottilie, her orphaned niece, as the new ingredient. The Captain suggests, ' ... now bring the pairs into contact; A will go over to D, C to B, without our being able to say who first left the other' (Goethe, 1809/1994: 34). The Captain and Ottilie will get together, both being single and unattached, and Eduard will thus be thrown back together in the company of his wife.

Their amiable analysis does not work out. It is the husband, Eduard, who is forcibly attracted to Ottilie, while Charlotte becomes intensely involved with the Captain. The quartet — and especially the marriage — is put under unbearable strain.

What is most remarkable in this plain-speaking novel is the chaotic nature of its emotional progression. The science of chemistry is valued at the start of the text, but, as the situation develops, a more powerful force becomes evident — alchemy. With Eduard at the height of his enchantment with Ottilie, and his wife, Charlotte, enthralled by the Captain, Eduard happens to find himself outside his wife's bedroom door and knocks for admittance. 'Her first thought was that, "it might, it must be the Captain"' but she is wrong, it is her husband, who says, 'I have vowed I shall kiss your shoe before the morning' (Goethe, 1809/1994: 78).

Both are in the grip of a passionate attachment to another person, but here the husband and wife find their way to each other by accident, and while they seduce each other they imagine those others by whom they are captivated. 'By lamplight, then, in a twilight, the heart's desires and the imagination at once asserted their rights over reality. Eduard held Ottilie in his arms; now closer, now receding, the Captain hovered before Charlotte's soul; and thus absent and present in the queerest fashion were intermingled, in excitement and delight' (Goethe, 1809/1994: 79).

More importance is attached by the characters in the story to the province of the imagination, than to the science of reality. Signifiers of fate begin to exert a powerful influence. A glass, which by chance happens to be engraved with the initials of Eduard and Ottilie, is thrown into the air during a ceremony to mark the laying of the foundation stone of a new house built on the estate, and ordinarily it would have fallen and smashed but someone on the scaffold caught the glass and so it never fell. At great cost Eduard buys it, and he drinks from it every day to re-affirm his hopes for a relationship with Ottilie. '[I]n the uncertainty of life,' begs Eduard, 'leave a heart struggling between hope and fear at least some sort of guiding star that it can look to, even if not steer by' (Goethe, 1809/1994: 113).

The alchemical influences proliferate. A visiting gentleman and his companion notice Ottilie's illogical aversion to a particular pathway on the estate and want to try an experiment. ' ... I cannot possibly leave here without having that beautiful child try the oscillations too' (Goethe, 1809/1994: 195). They set out the 'golden rings, marcasites, and other metallic substances' (Goethe, 1809/1994: 195), and first Charlotte and then Ottilie suspend the pendulum over the array of ingredients. With Charlotte there is no result, but with Ottilie, ' ... at once the dangling metal was seized, really as if in a whirlpool, and veered to one side or the other, according to what new substances were placed below, now in a circle, now in straight lines, just as the gentleman's companion might have hoped, in a way exceeding all his hopes' (Goethe, 1809/1994: 196).

One could not ask for a more scientific writer than Goethe yet it is alchemy that he invokes in his manufacture of fiction precisely because of its bluster, its downright lying and illusion-making — in other words, its magic. These qualities of magic are inherent in alchemy: the altering of the appearance of the ingredients, the changing of the onlooker's perception, the obstruction, the deliberate hiding of the truth. The self-delusion, the trickery of alchemy are more aligned to the behaviour of the human mind, deep in its own cave, than the always-predictable, immutable processes of chemistry.

In short, chemistry is physical while alchemy is metaphysical; and the novel is a metaphysical creature.

Kundera saw what the problem was. 'But how can *uncontrolled* imagination be integrated into the novel,' he asked, 'which by definition is supposed to be a lucid examination of existence? How can such disparate elements be united? That calls for a real alchemy!' (Kundera, 1986/2005: 83).

The alchemists, in their earliest manifestation, claimed it was an art that translated the inferior into the superior, that it was capable of transforming a mundane material, usually a common metal, into a valuable one — often gold. Francis Bacon tells us about a certain Sir Edward Dyer who travelled all the way to Germany to observe 'Kelley the alchemist'. On Dyer's return he hastened to the dinner table of the Lord of Canterbury to report what he had seen, and

> … turning to the Archbishop, [he] said ; ... *I saw Master Kelley put of the base metal into the crucible, and after it was set a little upon the fire, and a very small quantity of the medicine put in, and stirred with a stick of wood, it came forth in great proportion perfect gold, to the touch, to the hammer, to the test.* (Bacon, 1905: 886)

Today — especially given the Internet — it is still easy to find those who are excited to believe all these stories are true: a certain Reginald Merton, for instance, in an article on the Alchemy Lab website (http://www.alchemylab.com/history_of_alchemy.htm) lists an army of alchemists and what he believes to have been their certain, proven achievements, 'Raymond Lully made gold for the King of England. George Ripley gave a hundred thousand pounds of alchemical gold to the Knights of Rhodes... Gustavus Adolphus of Sweden had an enormous number of gold pieces coined... by an unknown man under the protection of the king'. Reginald argues that 'Only a very few adepts knew of the essential agent, the sublime heat of the soul, which fuses the emotions, consumes the prison of leaden form and allows entry into the higher world'.

The connection with myth making and deception means that my figure of the writer-as-alchemist is a close cousin to Lewis Hyde's trickster. In his long excavation of this cultural figure, *Trickster Makes This World* (1998), Hyde describes the trickster as, 'master of the kind of creative deception that, according to a long tradition, is a pre-requisite of art' (Hyde, 2008: 17).

The writer-as-alchemist, therefore, is my analogy, and this its thesis: that the manufacture of fiction requires the writer to take the base materials of life, whether they are unusual or commonplace, and ei-

---

Writing exercise no. 6: 'Gathering'

Start work — gather a pile of ingredients: the incidents, the setting, the characters, the buildings, the animals. Some of these materials will be used and others won't. Some will be used and thrown away. Some will have to be specifically sought out, half way through.

To 'gather' these ingredients might involve buying or borrowing books, or it might entail foreign travel, or perhaps you will only have to sit with a pen and notebook and remember events from your past. It might involve consulting car manuals or observing the habits of a wild animal on Youtube, or writing down observations on how people behave when they're waiting for trains. It might involve an in-depth exploration of medical advances in the 17th century, or the conceiving of a river system set in the future, when there is zero rainfall. Whichever is the case, it's the significant and attractive details that will offer the richest rewards.

You can't do enough 'gathering' — your novel will change and develop; it will find its way of giving its pleasures to your readers, but its success will depend on a rich gathering process.

---

ther turn them into gold, or make with them the Philosopher's Stone, or mix them to concoct the elixir of life.

How do we prepare ourselves for this task and how do we train ourselves in this art?

The work of the alchemist is to find and gather ingredients, then to mix and process them, or separate them out and keep them apart, subtly manipulate the elements, apply intense pressure, create explosions, conjure up magical transformations, hide trickery, manufacture bluff and thereby create belief, in order to make something apparently of great value and thus fiction extends its promise, to transform.

1. Gathering

Our first task is to harvest materials or ingredients; this is the essential (even if unconscious) precursor to the fictive process.

For *What The Children Saw* I will gather up memories of my children's imaginative games. We have all been children and know the common sights: the sheets and blankets thrown over sofas and chairs to make a den, the understairs cupboard transformed into a cave, the camp built of branches and foliage in the garden, the tower made of bricks, the toy cars parked in rows. They are evidence of children making up stories for themselves. The duration and intensity of such imaginative games confirm the compulsive attraction of storytelling.

I have fifteen years of such memories (in later years seeing only glimpses, overheard from a distance, because with older children an adult presence brings shame and breaks the spell) and I wish to construct for both the adult and the child reader a similar experience, of entering a game — a story — that is so compelling one never wishes to leave. So my base materials are both pedestrian and magical at the same time.

How does the novelist then take these base materials and make them valuable? It is the same question, in *A Portrait of the Artist as a Young Man* (1916), that Stephen asks the Dean, 'What is that beauty which the artist struggles to express from lumps of earth' (Joyce, 1916/2000: 154)?

We have our base materials: a scruffy assembly of ingredients, inert, but full of possibility, imbued with emotions as yet unrealized. So — what next?

2. Mixing together

Carol Shields starts her novel *The Stone Diaries* with a recipe for Malvern pudding and this puts her text on the right footing immediately for the purposes of this analogy. The mixture of ingredients — and also how you grind them, to get at the detail, how you stir them, heat them, apply pressure to them in order to join them together — is the issue here.

First of all we have one fat, greedy woman. 'Mercy Stone weighs forty stone' (Shields, 1993/2008: 33) was chanted as a skipping rhyme by the foundlings at the orphanage where Mercy Goodwill was brought up, and we learn that 'Eating was as close to heaven as my mother ever came' (Shields, 1993/2008: 1). Mixed with her, at-

tached to her, is the opposite quality in her husband, Cuyler Goodwill, a slender male, 'short of stature, small-boned and neat' (Shields,
1993/2008: 17), also described as 'a runt' (Shields, 1993/ 2008: 24)
and, to complement her appetite, he is a dainty eater even though he
works in a quarry, 'A pick-and-nibble fellow, she calls him, able to take
his food or leave it' (Shields, 1993/2008: 1).

Opposites attract. The minus qualities in his character are fixing
strongly to the positive values in hers. The glue is irony.

I can immediately seize on this, and use the shape of it for *What
The Children Saw*. In the first part of *The Stone Diaries* Carol Shields
brings us to the birth of her narrator and I, too, want to bring someone to life. But *What The Children Saw* is an Easter story; I want to
bring my character back from the dead. It is the story of the resurrection of a deceased grandparent.

I have two houses, on either side of the graveyard. What if, in
one house, there are plenty of grandparents available, and therefore
a rich supply of Easter eggs, while on the other side, there is none?
No grandparents, because they are all dead and gone. Now I have to
think how it could work the other way: in order to tie these two sets of
children together in an ironic double-bond, what could the children
without grandparents *have*, which their neighbours *don't* have?

To look for any possible answer, I continue to read *The Stone Diaries* and find more ironic oppositions arranged in her characters. Cuyler Goodwill is sexually charged. 'The tidal motion of sexual longing
filled him to the brim' (Shields, 1993/2008: 33) and 'he wants to bury
himself in her exalting abundance' (Shields, 1993/2008: 34) whereas
Mercy is sexually inert. ' ... he knew that Mercy Stone's ardour was
of a quality inferior to his own' (Shields, 1993/2008: 34) reports
the narrator, Daisy, and she goes on to describe how 'The potency
and fragrance of erotic love that overwhelmed him in his twenty-
sixth year was answered by Mercy with mild bewilderment' (Shields,
1993/2008: 33). The 'minus' in her connects with the 'plus' in him.

What other ingredients are selected? There is quite a collection
of things in that cavernous belly of Mercy's. Although the Malvern
pudding itself, the stale bread and the sweet blackcurrants, 'A warm
sponge soaking up color' (Shields, 1993/2008: 2) will not make it,

there is plenty of other stuff that does go in. 'One day, alone in the kitchen, she consumed an entire loaf between noon and supper' (Shields, 1993/2008: 6). And, 'she imagines the soft dough entering the bin of her stomach, lining that bitter bloated vessel with a cottony warmth' (Shields, 1993/2008: 6).

There is not only food in that stomach, but pain and discomfort, caused possibly by indigestion. At night 'she's risen from her sleep and dosed herself with Bishop's Citrate of Magnesia' (Shields, 1993/2008: 5). And there is more pain and discomfort. 'Her abdominal walls have continued to cramp and heave all spring ... She experiences scalding attacks of flatulence, especially at night' (Shields, 1993/2008: 6).

Carol Shields has made the woman huge, and the things in her belly become huge as well — the food, the hunger, the pain, the flatulence, and of course, the most important thing of all — the narrator, Daisy, a foetus about to be born.

Another recipe — another mixture of ingredients to which careful processes have been applied — is the cast of characters recruited to witness this birth: 'Life is an endless recruiting of witnesses. It seems we need to be observed in our postures of extravagance or shame, we need attention paid to us' (Shields, 1993/2008: 36).

The newly weds, Mercy and Cuyler, are given neighbours who are at the other end of the childbirth tunnel. Mrs Flett is 'half-crazed by menopause and loneliness' (Shields, 1993/2008: 37) and she is fed up with her husband's advances ... 'I am not willing' (Shields, 1993/2008: 16) she imagines saying to him, to deflect his unromantic, prosaic demands for sex, while she listens, jealously, to Mercy's husband saying how much he loves her. 'I love you,' she heard young Cuyler Goodwill say to his immense, bloated wife, Mercy. 'Oh how I love you, and with all my heart.' (Shields, 1993/2008: 16).

If Mercy has something that Clarentine Flett longs for, then the reverse is also true. Mercy wants nothing more than the cold box given to Clarentine by *her* husband. Each has something the other wants — like a double hand clasp — and the joinery used again is irony. (Shields frequently uses irony to bind together her ingredients. Later on, in the two sets of letters written on pages 50–8, while one correspondent thanks Cuyler for providing money, the other correspondent, Marcus Flett, is begging his father to send money.)

On the day of the birth of the narrator, a character called 'the old Jew' enters stage left, with his 'high-pitched yipping' (Shields, 1993/2008: 19). He is a picture of madness in this sane, almost suburban setting and it adds that note of danger to the proceedings. 'The voice is demented; it has the creak of terror in it' (Shields, 1993/2008: 21).

Carol Shields has also stirred another set of ingredients into this opening sequence: the past, present and future. The future, in the shape of the narrator, Daisy, who has travelled back in time to describe things she cannot possibly have seen or known about — among them, her own birth. An imagined future is Cuyler's hardly dared-for dream of having children and 'a more commodious house, lit in the evenings with brighter lamps' (Shields, 1993/2008: 35). The present and the future are wrapped together in the shape of Mercy's cooking of the Malvern pudding which the narrator has the authority to withdraw from us at the end, using past, present and future tenses: 'Where, you ask, is the Malvern pudding, weighted with its ancient stone? It has been set aside, as has my mother's cookery book. They will not be seen again in this story' (Shields, 1993/2008: 38). The present is also evident in Cuyler's walk back home from work to confront the scene of his wife's labour, and in the cast of characters 'invited to participate in a moment of history. History indeed! As though this paltry slice of time deserves such a name. Accident, not history, has called us together, and what an assembly we make' (Shields, 1993/2008: 39). And the past is there, in the extensive telling of Mercy's lack of history, her upbringing in the foundling home, and in the convincing portrayal of Cuyler's past, 'the chill and meagreness of his parents' house' (Shields, 1993/2008: 28).

Thus it seems like all of time itself is brought together for this exact moment, which she describes as a 'clamour of inadequacy and portent,' to witness whatever comes out of the mixture of ingredients which have been mashed up together in Mercy's stomach.

The grip (with irony the atomic force that binds the elements) creates an inward pressure, and the tighter the elements are bound together the more it loads up the force of the explosion to come.

And yet how disparate and conflicting is this mixture Carol Shields has concocted — she seems to admit, 'I long to bring symmetry to the various discordant elements' (Shields, 1993/2008: 23) — but of course, in this instance as in so many others in this novel (when she pretends to observe her own birth, when she puts fake photographs in the middle of the book to increase its authority as an autobiography), the author is a liar. She does not 'long to bring symmetry' at all, she has deliberately chosen such discordant elements. Indeed, they are her chosen form of symmetry.

And I have left until last the biggest opposites that she arranges together: the oil and the water, the two that never can mix — life and death. She presses them up against each other just as tightly as she possibly can, 'the clout of death and the wriggling foolishness of birth' (Shields, 1993/2008: 40). She bangs their heads together, in one sharp instant, to give this story its life. Mercy will die in the act of childbirth.

The art of alchemy defines one of its processes as exhalation — the escape of a gas, an invisible thing, from the mixture. Carol Shields grinds up her mixture, and achieves this exhalation. In order to create (literally out of the last breath of the dying Mercy) the beginning of the story, the birth of the narrator in this *faux* autobiography, she writes:

> It's this wing-beat of breath I reach out for. Even now I claim it absolutely. I insist upon its literal volume and vapors, for however hard I try I can be sure of nothing else in the world but this — the fact of her final breath, the merest trace of it lingering in the room like snow or sunlight, burning, freezing against my sealed eyelids and saying: open, open. (Shields, 1993/2008: 40)

The exhalation is the start of the story. She creates it with poetic force. The 'wingbeat' gives the sound and the feeling of breath, of a slight edge of fear, of taking flight, of vertigo. The 'volume and the vapors' give us the sense of smoke, of the space that the story needs to unfold, opening up in front of us.

Even within the body of this paragraph there is the determined bringing together of discordant, opposite ingredients. The large and the small, signified by the world (huge, overwhelming) bumped up against 'the merest trace' of breath and a newborn's eyelids (tiny, fragile). The cold and the hot — snow and sunlight. A beginning and an ending — the last breath is the end of Mercy's life but the start of Daisy's. That opening is magically described in the command given by the narrator to the baby's 'sealed eyelids' and she speaks them out loud, in direct speech, so we can hear them, 'open, open.' It is the perfect beginning, and the perfect ending also.

So much for the art of mixing elements together. It can be seen that it is not only a question of selecting the ingredients that will cling to each other, but also it is that old alchemists' trick of applying pressure: leaning down hard on the pestle as it grinds the ingredients even finer to get to the detail and to create the forces of attraction which will combine the elements, and provide the exhalation, to create the genesis of the story.

In *What The Children Saw*, I am only halfway to creating the ironic bond between my two sets of children. Then it occurs to me — what if, on one side of the graveyard, there is an only child, without siblings, but with plenty of grandparents, while on the other side you have three siblings, who have each other, but no grandparents?

I have gathered together some new ingredients for the opening sequence of *What The Children Saw*. I will not open with the church porch, or the graveyard, or the children in their homes. This material might be thrown away, or it might come later.

Instead, I am mixing the ingredients with an eye on how they will bind together. On each side, the one party has what the other lacks: Megan lacks siblings but has eight grandparents (because they have divorced and remarried); and the siblings lack grandparents but have each other. I will begin the story by choosing incidents that will illustrate this ironic bond: it is Easter day, and I call into play the Easter egg as a symbol of resurrection. I want to write this out, to see if it will stick.

It was Easter Sunday; and games were forbidden. An unearthly quiet hung over both houses — no running feet, no slamming doors — and Megan went to wait for her grandparents at the spot where they would park their cars. She was joined by the other three children who came down their own driveway: Emma rolling like a boulder, the slap of each footfall marking her out, and the Billies like spiders with their legs and arms moving continually.

'Happy Easter,' said Emma to Megan.

'Hey, and you. Happy Easter,' said Megan.

The Billies scrambled up to find a hiding place in the rhododendron bushes, while Megan and Emma waited more conspicuously on the pavement, meandering back and forth.

A small red car dragged its exhaust pipe along the ground like a broken, metallic tail. The Billies, their limbs threaded among the rhododendron's branches, shrank back, not to be seen. Emma stayed where she was, with Megan. She only climbed substantial trees, and anyway she didn't ever care to be hidden.

When the vehicle stopped Megan leaned through the driver's window to greet the occupants, before they climbed out to examine the broken exhaust pipe. There was nothing they could do. They opened the boot and took hold of two Easter eggs and handed them to Megan, who found that Emma was at her shoulder, breathing heavily. Emma took the eggs off her, one by one, and shook them, to hear the answering rattle which told her they had sweets inside, before she politely handed them back.

Writing exercise no. 7: 'Lists'

Stand your characters next to each other and list in which ways they are similar and in which ways they are opposite to each other, both in terms of their physical attributes and their character traits, and their deep, unavoidable characters. It makes a difference to put a rich person next to a poor one, a person with good table manners next to a sloppy eater, a brave person next to a timid one. Similarly, to put people next to each other who have similar traits of character sponsors something else. Once you have made these lists, swap them all around, play God. And watch out for the nuggets of story, of incident, that come to mind as a consequence of this exercise. Make a note of these incidents.

David and Ben, obscured in the leafy shadows, also measured the size of the Easter eggs, the colour and extravagance of the wrappings, their apparent weight.

Megan escorted her grandparents up the driveway at a slow, slow pace, while the others remained behind. In a few minutes she returned and with her she brought three mini-eggs, as consolation for the others. Emma and Ben rubbed and picked at the silver wrapping which clung to the sweaty chocolate until they could pop them in their mouths. David saved his for later, when the others would have finished.

There was an interlude, which dragged on while the next pair of grandparents failed to arrive. Nothingy sorts of things happened: Ben tried to dig a hole but David stopped him. David climbed to the fourth branch of the copper beech. Megan complained that her feet hurt. Emma folded and folded again the scrap of silver paper which had encased the mini-egg she'd been given. If it were a magic egg, it would reappear when you rubbed the paper between your palms like this ... it would be good as new; she could unwrap it again, eat it, once more rub the silver paper in her hands and hey-presto, there'd be another, and again she'd eat ...

3. Separating out

We have looked at ingredients mixed together, but what about the opposite? Alchemy provides not only for mixing together, but also for separation, for dissociation, segregation — the pressure applied in the opposite direction to keep elements apart. 'Towards the effecting of works, all that man can do is to put together or put asunder natural bodies. The rest is done by Nature working within' (Bacon, 1905: 259).

Strikingly, in the first 40 pages of *The Stone Diaries*, the alchemy of segregation is brought to bear on the business of the pregnancy. Carol Shields has stormed in disguised as Daisy and with none of the many declarations of truth or untruth that she gives to other matters she pushes apart the two most important strands in this part of the story: the pregnancy, and the parents' knowledge of the pregnancy. Mercy does not have a clue she is pregnant, therefore neither does Cuyler.

And yet she is about to give birth. It is the reason, of course, Carol Shields has made her so fat, in order to construct the logic of this invention, so that we might believe such an incredible thing.

Why has she kept this knowledge of the pregnancy from her characters, but allowed it to us?

First, because it brings dramatic irony into play, which has an adhesive quality in narrative, as in life. When the information possessed by us, the reader, is greater than that of the characters in the story, it creates in us a sense of privilege. It has a delicious narcissistic quality, this spell that is cast when dramatic irony is summoned. We can assume the all-seeing, all-knowing presence of a God; we can feel ourselves, irrationally, more clever than the characters ... It creates an area within this story that we have earned by our understanding, by our perception, our prescience. It appears exclusive to us because the characters in the story are excluded. Dramatic irony also creates forward impetus — it heavily tilts the story, because we wish to hurry the story along so that we can arrive at the moment when the characters find out what we already know. It is a rich narrative gift and it must be delivered silently, without our being told. There are other narrative conceits that Carol Shields cheerfully admits to but not this one, because if she does so we will see that we are not God, after all — she is — and our pleasure would be diminished.

Mercy and her own pregnancy are kept apart in order to ferment dramatic irony, but there is a second reason for separating them out: Carol Shields wishes to create what would be called in the vocabulary of the alchemist an explosion. In the language of the novelist it might be described as a surprise.

It works by sleight of hand (the skills of a magician are necessary to the work of the alchemist) and the prerequisite to this particular sleight of hand is the keeping of those two elements apart: the pregnancy, and the parents' knowledge of the pregnancy.

This is how it works. Carol Shields has mixed together two characters: the male, Cuyler, mounts the female copiously, energetically, and the female ... well, submits. Mercy's stomach is filled with food, and pain, and flatulence, and a baby — our narrator Daisy. Gradually, we become aware — since it is never mentioned — that Mercy does not know she is pregnant, and neither does Cuyler. Not even today, on the day of the birth of a baby that purportedly will live long enough to write this book, do they know. We are allowed to understand that there is a baby in that vast stomach because it is the baby herself who is telling us the story of the circumstances of her birth.

As Mercy puts aside the Malvern pudding, as she leans over the table with her first contractions, with the hysterical calling for help of the old Jew, and with Cuyler's sunny, carefree walk home from work, we are involved in the construction of a surprise for Mercy and a surprise for Cuyler, and for the neighbouring Flett family ... a surprise for everyone except us: that a baby will arrive soon. Daisy is about to be born. We, the readers, are gleeful at the prospect of seeing the explosion. But, and here is the sleight of hand, while Carol Shields appears to amaze and delight us with the delivery of this surprise to these characters (and so we are watching, transfixed), she is, meanwhile, delivering a different explosion to us, the reader.

That explosion is the death of Mercy. The detonation goes off right under our noses.

The others have had some intimation, a warning, that something is up. Mercy has the terrific bouts of pain. The old Jew has run for the doctor. The Flett woman has gone over to help. But we are to walk in on the scene — what we know will be this startling appearance of a baby — and for this moment the author puts us in the company of the least forewarned, the most to-be-surprised among the cast of characters: Cuyler Goodwill, the husband so desperately, erotically in love with his wife, and the man who is already dreaming of children filling a larger, warmer, more brightly lit house than this one he's walking into. He is:

> ... hungry for the supper already prepared, eager for whatever tenderness the evening will bring. His small dark face and sinewy body burst through his back door, the tune he has been whistling dying on his lips as he falls upon this scene of chaos, his house with its unanticipated unbearable human crowding, a strange sharp scent rising to his nostrils, and a high, rhythmic cry of lamentation — where is this coming from, where? — these terrifying vowel sounds, iii-yyeeee, spiralling upward and joining the derangement of linen and of air, at the

> center of which lies his wife — on the blood drenched kitchen couch, its gathered cretonne cover — my mother, her mountainous body stilled, her eyes closed. (Shields, 1993/2008: 38)

'*Stilled, her eyes closed*' … Bang, goes the detonation. It is so close up. The body 'stilled, her eyes closed' is the first shockwave, because we are expecting tears in those eyes, and the frightened smile of the new mother. Instead, Mercy is dead? And then:

> 'eclampsia,' Dr Spears says solemnly, pulling a sheet — no, not a sheet but a tablecloth — up over her face, and staring at her father with severity. 'Almost certainly eclampsia'. (Shields, 1993/2008: 38)

The doctor's voice says, 'eclampsia' whereas it should be saying, 'It's a girl.' The sheet not as it should be, drawn around Mercy's enormous breasts to protect her modesty, but instead drawn up all the way over her face, in the common gesture signifying death.

A cliché is used because this detonation needs to be quick, and sure. The writer pretends to correct herself — 'not a sheet, no, a tablecloth … ' — and with this correction she stamps her authority on the text. We have been smartly smacked in the face. Carol Shields has shown us who is in control — she is. We are ready to believe every word she tells us.

Thus she demonstrates that we must look for opportunities for separation if we want to create dramatic irony and invigorate the alchemy of our narrative.

In *What The Children Saw*, the girls will make a deal. Megan is an only child, and Emma will lend her two brothers to Megan, to play with for three hours. In exchange, Emma asks for half of Megan's second-largest Easter egg. If we keep the knowledge of this deal secret from the boys (the Billies as I have decided to call them), then the alchemy will begin to simmer:

> Emma and Megan drifted together, as if by accident. The billies, a little way off, could hear the girls' quiet, mysterious murmuring without being able to make out what they were saying.
> 'Two hours,' mumbled Emma.
> 'Three?'

'How *big* then?'

Megan's instinct was to be generous, to give to Emma all her Easter eggs, her whole heart and mind and all her possessions, her life on a plate, because she wanted nothing less in return from Emma, but it didn't work like that. It took her some moments of staring blankly, kicking the pavement, tugging at her clothes, to recover. 'Not the very biggest,' she replied, 'but you can choose half, of any one you like *below* that. Just half of it.'

'For three hours?'

'Yes. Alone, though. Without you.'

'The whole egg.'

'No, half.'

'Deal?'

'For half.'

'Deal?'

'Yes, deal,' Megan echoed back. The two girls touched their closed fists which did for a handshake. It wasn't as complicated and intimate as the handshake Emma performed with her brothers: after the closed fists they would slap their palms, top and bottom, clasp each other's fingers, twiddle their thumbs. It rankled with Megan to be excluded from this ritual. 'Don't tell them, though,' she said, as Emma wandered off.

'Course not.'

'Really, don' t tell them.'

'I won't.'

'Promise.'

'I won't tell them.'

The Billies do not know they have been sold. This is my separation. However, it strikes me that an opportunity exists to create the separation in a different way, to lever apart different elements of the story, to greater effect. If Emma breaks her word and tells the boys about the deal (and she always tells them, because this happens all the time) then it is Megan whom we feel sorry for. Our sense of pity for Megan as an only child will be compounded by our witnessing the boys' knowledge that she's had to pay for them to play with her.

David and Ben were kicking each other's shins. Emma pulled them apart. 'Megan's got you both for three hours,' she said brutally.

'When?'

'This afternoon.'

'How much?'

'One… one bite. Each. A small one.'

They stared at her, distrustful.

Writing exercise no. 8: 'Keeping apart'

In the last writing exercise, I asked you to stand your characters next to each other and define or create opposites and similarities. This time, stand not only your characters together, but also the incidents that happen. Make a list or draw a diagram describing who knows what about any particular incident. Deliberately strike out characters from knowing about an incident — especially if they should, by rights, be the first to have known about them — and see what happens. Also, do the reverse: allow a stranger knowledge of an incident. This exercise will, by itself, propagate more story. It will create surprises and generate dramatic irony. Some of your most powerful sequences will come out of your use of this exercise.

The mixing together of ingredients: siblings, an only child, Easter eggs, grandparents. The separation of ingredients: Megan not knowing that the boys know she has paid for their company. Both are designed to work towards an exhalation: the birth of the story, created by Megan's idea for a game she might play with the Billies. And here I need to foreshadow it, and create in the text the genesis of the game:

> Megan was alone again, and back in the rut of waiting … Grandparents were a bore. The others had romantic notions about them, but if they had some of their own, they'd know. She fell into a reverie. What would she do with the billies, later? Three hours, she had, for something good. There was, suddenly, a picture in her mind: the sideboard in the dining room in Emma's house, its cupboard door opening, and the dark recess within — the unknown. Numerous strange objects there … a funeral urn, she was sure. Or more than one. Her own hand, white as a ghost's, reached in …
>
> How many stories started with a door opening, she wondered? Millions.

She pushed the idea away — no. If she suggested such a thing, the billies would think she was mad.

4. The art of logic

We can do anything we choose with our characters. We are Gods playing with their fates. But we have to be able to suspend the disbelief of our readers, and in its place create belief, if we want to enchant them. To create such a belief, we have to attend to the logic, however fantastic the scenario. (The absence of logic, especially, should be logical.) In *What The Children Saw*, if I am to create belief in the story, it should make sense.

We are so thoroughly caught up in the alchemy of Carol Shields' detonation only because of the lavish attention she gives to the logic of the situation. In the case of Mercy Goodwill's death, Shields' embrace of logic is proven if we follow upstream the moment-by-moment identification of two separate channels of cause and effect. When we follow Cuyler into the room, the sights and sounds that Carol Shields arranges for us are equally logical in a death scene and a birth scene: the chaos, the strange smell, the cry of lamentation, the 'iii-yeee', the mess of linen, the bloodied couch ... it is only when we reach that word 'stilled,' and we see Mercy's eyes not open but closed, that we experience the explosion and realize this is her death bed. In a trice, unthinking, we trace the logic backwards from the word 'eclampsia'. The sights and sounds that Carol Shields has described in order to warn us of Daisy's imminent birth are the same sights and sounds that will make sense given the fact, now, of Mercy's *death*. The sheer size of Mercy is a central plank in this logic. It is the reason why she might not know of her own pregnancy; and eclampsia, the reason the author gives for Mercy's death, is a condition commonly ascribed to overweight mothers. Mercy's refusal to go to the doctor is another visible strut in the construction of this logic: eclampsia is diagnosed via high blood pressure and a visit to the doctor would easily have told Mercy she was in danger. The pain, the flatulence ... all these are symptomatic of eclampsia *and* pregnancy. Because we find that everything fits, because the logic is evident, we therefore approve, and believe.

The romantically named Arnoldus de Nova Villa, alchemist and philosopher, correctly divined the importance of the relationship between alchemy and logic. ' ... therefore no body should approach to this art [alchemy], unlesse he has heard before some Logick, which teaches to distinguish truth from falsehood, and withall the naturall art which teaches the things of nature, and the property of the elements, otherwise he troubles his minde and body and life in vaine' (De Nova Villa, 1986).

In order to underpin the bluster and the trickery of the alchemical process, and in order to create his effect, the alchemist must engage in a love-affair with logic. It might be only a semblance of logic but it must appear watertight.

The magician, just like the alchemist, must be a devotee of logic, but must work towards the opposite effect. The magician knows that to pull a rabbit out of a hat is not enough — is nothing, in fact — without obscuring, or masking, the logic of how it got there. The aim of the magician is to deliver a surprise and arouse in the audience the reaction, 'I don't believe it! What an incredible trick!'. The novelist must deliver the surprise and at the same time sponsor in the reader the opposite reaction, 'I believe it, I *see* ... '. This is the critical difference between the magician and the writer-as-alchemist. For the writer, the evidence of logic — its display, the sight of it — is essential if we are to believe the story as being 'real'.

It is not that we do not understand that the most blinding coincidences and accidents of fate happen in real life. They happen all the time. But a trick, a twist without logic, in fiction, has no currency because it is the easy way out for an author and does nothing for us but unmask the author-as-puppeteer, whereas for the magician, it *is* his currency and it *is* the difficult thing to do.

The novelist has to do as much work to show the logic that delivers the surprise as the magician does to obscure it. And yet to show the logic will give away the surprise. This is the anomaly that the fiction writer must deal with, in one way or another.

5. Still on the art of logic

In *The Secret Scripture* (2008) by Sebastian Barry there are two detonations; one of them works and one of them does not. The detonation that fails, I am willing to guess, cost him the Booker Prize of 2008 and was responsible for the extraordinary sight of the Costa prize chairman explaining that they were making this book their winner even though it had 'something wrong with the ending.'

The Secret Scripture is narrated by two different voices: that of Roseanne Clear, a very old lady who has been falsely incarcerated in a lunatic asylum ever since she gave birth to an illegitimate baby in 1957, and that of Dr Grene, who is in charge of Roscommon Regional Mental Hospital, where she has ended up. The hospital is in the process of closing down, and throughout the story Grene finds out more and more about his elderly patient, how she was ill-served by her family and sectioned when she was in fact perfectly sane. He finds out about the infant she bore, as she crouched in 'a nest of boulders' (Barry, 2008: 262) in the middle of a storm. The newborn was taken from her breast while she slept, out in the open. She awoke and 'there was blood and the skin and cord and the placenta. I started to my feet. I was as dizzy and weak as a newborn foal myself. Where was my baby?' (Barry, 2008: 264).

No one knows what happened to the baby. Dr Grene is the only person who wants to take the trouble to find out.

Towards the end of the book Dr Grene travels to an orphanage in Bexhill, Surrey, to track down the child who was taken from Roseanne's breast so long ago. He is put in a room with the relevant documents. 'The child's name was William Clear, born of Roseanne Clear, waitress ... The child was given to Mr and Mrs Grene of Padstow, Cornwall, in 1945' (Barry, 2008: 289).

He himself *is* that child — this is the detonation. Immediately, quick as a tidal surge, we reach upstream for a seam of logic that brought us here ... but we search in vain. There is nothing. Sebastian Barry thought to pull off this detonation, this surprise, in the same way as might a magician, by obscuring the logic. His argument for doing it in this way might have been that it is how life happens: sometimes we get these vulnerable, uncertain places in the unfolding of events, and a novel that is true-to-life must therefore contain them.

Another reason might have been that to have shown any part of the logic in advance would have spoilt the surprise, but that is exactly what makes it so difficult to pull off a good surprise in fiction. It is sleight of hand that must obscure the logic, it is not enough simply to leave it out. So, that is the art required: to disguise it in such a way that we see it, but do not see it.

Writing exercise no. 9: 'The woodland glade'

For once and for all, dispose of the phrase 'show not tell', and forget all about it; it creates confusion and despair. But it's important to understand what this phrase is trying to tell you, in a misguided way. The phrase is asking you to create a display of logic that demands the involvement of the reader in working something out, however gentle and small scale that thing might be. You will do this by either leaving out the 'cause' part of the logic, or the 'effect' part of the logic. To achieve this end, you can 'tell' anything you like, and you can 'show' anything you like.

Draw a circle, which represents a woodland glade. Around the edges of the circle draw some trees, and one or two paths that lead into the woodland glade.

In the circle that describes the woodland glade, write something you wish your reader to know. Let's say, for instance, it's the fact that 'Emily is sad.' Once you've written it down in the circle, banish yourself from the woodland glade. Only your reader is allowed to go into the glade, and it's your job, as the writer, to describe the trees, and the pathways around the edges, so that the reader will arrive at the woodland glade under their own steam. To do this, you can tell, you can show, you can make a list, you can do everything except enter that woodland glade yourself.

When your readers have found their way into it for themselves — and not before — then you are allowed to enter the woodland glade, and join them.

Choose what you tell, and choose what you show, to create a display of logic that demands the involvement of your reader.

In true life the surprise would have been gratifying. We would have shaken our heads in wonder at it. In fiction we feel cheated. We can see the author's hand working the characters. The illusion-making spell is broken. It is such a big trick that we feel doubly resentful.

In truth, this coincidence, which we would have accepted if it had been positioned at the beginning of the story, was of no consequence. The enormous power and beauty of this novel has already been dealt to us magnificently for 288 pages, with only a dozen left to go. It does not matter who the child is. For the duration of a few lines the bubble bursts, but any reader with a heart will mend the bubble themselves and carry on.

The artist and writer Sebastian Horsley purposefully travelled half way across the world to have himself crucified and did not die but merely fainted. Instead, at home, in his bed, he died by accident. He loomed over me once at the junction of Wardour Street and Meard St, his tie a huge eggshell blue triangle at his neck, the suit of clothes a rich silver, and he put it succinctly, 'The difference between fiction and non-fiction is that fiction has to make sense.'

Non-fiction writing has its logic-work done for it, and does not need to add up, whereas fiction-writing requires not only the invention of its logic, and that the logic should appear watertight (especially if the story proposes a nonsense world), but for its full powers to be invoked a novel also requires the author's delightful manipulation of logic on behalf of the reader — an artful display of logic.

This requires me to insist even further on the importance of logic.

6. Still more on the art of logic

The work of the alchemist Francis Bacon was wholly geared towards 'the inquisition of Causes, and the production of Effects... and I know it well, that there is an intercourse between Causes and Effects... ascending from experiments to the invention of Causes, and descending from Causes to the invention of new experiments' (Bacon, 1905: 92). Arriving from a different direction, I have come to appreciate the powerful influence of logic, and the manipulation of logic, on the art of composing fiction.

I sometimes walk at night on the moorland that stretches from the gates of my house for a distance of forty miles or so westward. When I return, and come down off the moor to approach what I think of (since to leave the moor is somewhat like arriving safely at the shore) as the inland pastures, where hedgerow, and wall, and tree cover are all different thicknesses of shadow, I am alerted to the presence of three or four owls at work in their various territories. They will be barn owls or little owls, and the screeches signify they are protecting territory and hunting: the terrifying sound is to frighten mice and voles, and make them move in the grass.

An owl's eyes have developed in a specific way to help them catch their prey at night. They are large, like massive tubular cameras, so big that they cannot swivel in their sockets as ours can (instead their heads turn). The iris has an extensive range, shrinking the entrance to the pupil to a pinprick but at night opening to allow the entire circumference of the eye to capture light. Their retinas have very few colour-sensitive cones, and this makes room for a higher density of the rods that detect black and white, which are more effective in gathering light. They have three eyelids: one for blinking, another which closes during sleep, and a third for cleaning. All these features have evolved to allow the eye to see in the dark almost as well as in the day.

The flatness of their faces, and the distance between their eyes, allows them to judge depth of field and more accurately locate their prey. The way they bob their heads up and down and from side to side increases this effect. They are judging distance, depth — position.

They are perfectly adapted to see, from a long way off, that movement in the grass.

They swoop silently, the tip of each feather is soft as down to allow noiseless flight. The owl is moving fast towards its prey but their eyes become less useful now, because they are adapted for long sight. The picture begins to blur.

The owl's sense of hearing takes over. The barn owl, in particular has a pronounced facial disc, like saucers around the eyes. They act like radar dishes to gather sound into the ear apertures. The apertures themselves (situated just behind the radar dishes) are asymmetrical, one side higher than the other, to allow for up-and-down location of the sound. If the vole moves backwards an inch, the sound comes from an inch lower, and the sound will arrive quicker at the right ear. If the vole darts forwards and the sound comes from an inch higher than before, the left ear hears it a fraction earlier. The owl has developed extraordinary ability in this; it can measure a difference in time between its ears of 0.00003 seconds.

Side to side movement is measured in the same way. The combination of signals is processed instantly in the owl's brain, on the wing. The owl keeps its facial disk pointing towards the sound, and follows. They have developed pinpoint spatial awareness from the auditory signal.

Close to its prey, the owl stalls and reaches forward with its talons while keeping its facial disk precisely aimed at the sound.

For the last couple of feet, the owl *closes its eyes*. Their sense of sound is wholly accurate (and it allows them to catch prey under snow or under leaves), and this closing of their eyes just before impact implies — to my mind — a delicious gastronomy, a sense of bliss in its capturing food, that must come, surely, as a reward at this point.

As I walk home in the moonlight I hear two or three different owls, all up to the same thing. It stirs one's attachment to a landscape, that it is shared with such creatures.

The owls' confabulation of sound and vision to locate the slightest movement in the grass is an example of the way in which an individual species has developed specific skills in order to make use of the world that surrounds it.

We, mankind, have won extraordinary dominion over our surroundings, so what is our species-specific skill? In what area of the brain have we developed extraordinary ability? The answer is logic.

If the blood is poisoned and heats up in a fever, then we find out why, and stop it. If the car breaks down we will find out why and fix it. If the colour blue is too expensive to produce we will find a cheaper way to make it. If water is the only liquid that expands when frozen then we will take measures to protect ourselves from the damaging effects. If my wife's eyes are downcast when receiving her birthday gift

I must try and guess why. If a crumb of sodium buzzes around on the surface of water, we will do everything in our power to find out why and make use of it. Our every waking moment is, and has been — ever since the suffix 'sapiens' was added to our species nomenclature — dedicated to the enquiry into (and the engineering of) cause and effect, or logic.

Francis Bacon put a God-made-man at the centre of his universe and thought that everything was arranged to suit him, but I would put it the other way around, Man developed extraordinary skill at logic and thereby learned to use animals and plants of every kind to feed himself, provide shelter, clothing, food, medicine, to give him comfort and pleasure and to reduce his work. He learned to trap the wind in his sails and he altered the course of water to drive his mills. He worked out how the stars could give him directions, worked out how predicting the weather might help his farms.

All our science, art, observation, psychology, all our design, is the operation of logic's pulleys and levers.

It is one of the two skills uniquely well-developed in our species (I would like to mention the other one later): we observe a change, the slightest whisper of a change, and we race to find out why, and what caused that change, and what the consequences will be. This attribute is so finely tuned in our species that any change, however small, is, for us, *a movement in the grass.*

We ceaselessly measure how things change and why. We measure the extra pound of weight on our waist, or another grey hair. We measure the increase or decrease in our wealth. We measure the smallest alteration in our affection for our friends or family, as well as the apparent changes in their affection for us, and we fret about the reasons. Our brain is wired to measure change and the reasons for change and what we might do about it. Logic is how we work, and why we win, why we eat.

De Nova Villa was right and the novelist, charged with bringing the art of alchemy to the writing of fiction, is wise not only to deal in logic but to develop a great love for it, a passionate engagement with cause and effect, with change, and an understanding of how it might be manipulated and beautifully displayed in order to seize the attention of the reader. The skilful novelist takes delight in creating the movement in the grass that will transfix the reader.

In *Wuthering Heights* (1847), Emily Brontë gives us, first of all, Lockwood's account of Heathcliff: a violent, cold-hearted, disappointed man who murdered his own son and enslaved his daughter-in-law. The author then conjures a storm in order to force Lockwood into staying the night so she might describe him — quickly — going up to the attic bedroom and discovering Catherine's diary. This diary gives a different view of Heathcliff. As a boy, he was neither cold-hearted, nor disappointed, nor murderous, nor a bully. When the child diary-writer Catherine throws her book into the fireplace we learn that 'Heathcliff kicked his to the same place' (Brontë, 1847: 22). He is copying her; far from being an assertive bully he is a willing passenger. The diary continues. They hide together after she 'just fastened our pinafores together, and hung them up for a curtain' (Brontë, 1847: 22). The child Heathcliff suggests to the child Catherine, 'that we should appropriate the dairy woman's cloak, and have a scamper on the moors, under its shelter. A pleasant suggestion' (Brontë, 1847: 22). The child Heathcliff wants to please the child Catherine; in his love for her he is generous, optimistic, adventurous. And this is in spite of the fact that Heathcliff himself is ill treated, 'Poor Heathcliff!' Catherine's diary continues, 'Hindley calls him a vagabond, and won't let him sit with us, nor eat with us anymore; and he says, he and I must not play together, and threatens to turn him out of the house if we break his orders' (Brontë, 1847: 24).

Two different Heathcliffs are put in front of us, side by side: a vicious, 'unnmannerly wretch' (Brontë, 1847: 17) in his middle age, and an innocent, imaginative, loving child. It is a big gap — a big change. We are well and truly alerted. We swoop on this, we demand to know the logic of how and why such a change took place. How the one Heathcliff became the other. We begin to make our guesses; we start work immediately. The remaining 360 pages is our flight, at the end of which we have that full and complete understanding: Heathcliff changed to such an extent not so much due to his ill-treatment at the hands of others but because his perfect love for Catherine (when she unfairly changed into a different type of person) was rejected. A

Writing exercise no. 10: 'The accident'

A second exercise on the subject of logic, since it's such an important skill to master.

Conceive of a situation where an accident or crime is about to happen. For instance, a jealous sister is going to push her brother down the stairs. Walk your characters right up to the moment of the accident making it clear that the accident is about to happen. Our two children would be standing at the top of the stairs, and the sister's hand goes to the middle of her brother's back, ready to push.

Now — do not describe the accident, but instead leap forward in time, maybe one day later, or a week later, and conceive a further scene wherein it becomes clear to us, without being told, what did happen. For instance, the boy is no longer in the house. The girl has no-one to play with. And then change it — let's say that the girl's leg is in plaster, instead. By describing the 'effect' of cause-and-effect without describing the 'cause' part, you will create your reader's powerful involvement in the story.

---

brute like Heathcliff becomes a romantic hero for millions of readers because the logic is compelling: the scale of the change in Heathcliff, the extent to which he has become vicious, is the exact measure of the depth and ferocity of his love for Catherine — a girl who turned to dust in his fingers.

Emily Brontë engineered this section of the novel when Lockwood is narrator to be directly adjacent to the section when Catherine's diary is the narrator, and in this way she skips from one time to another and from one point-of-view to another in order to give us, at the outset of the novel, the 'effect' in 'cause-and-effect' and to a reader this is magical. It is the movement in the grass. We demand to know the cause so that we can join it to the effect. We swoop on the rest of the story, eat it up.

Ford Madox Ford, in *The Good Soldier* (1915), creates layer after layer of effect and cause in a similar way — each layer creating differences in our perception of his characters — by manipulating the point of view of the narration and by using his 'fireside' narrator to skip back and forth in time. It is the same manipulation of time and point-of-view, but executed in a more subtle and refined way.

In the analogy following this one, I will describe how a number of literary novelists use the same technique to construct an objective, a forward progression in their stories. This is what fiction-writing is: orchestrating a dance with logic; it is a display.

Monty Roberts, the rodeo champion, race-horse trainer and horse-whisperer, describes in his autobiography *The Man Who Listens To Horses,* how the dominant mare in a wild herd would discipline badly-behaved youngsters by aggressively driving them outside the group. Standing alone, some distance away, the youngster would become aware of the danger of his position. Predators would be looking to pick off any animal left unprotected, outside the group. The adolescent would submit, and beg to be let back in.

This psychology accounted for various inexplicable behaviours in horses. Monty's observations furnished him with a special ability to understand them and manipulate their behaviour. He described them as 'into-pressure' creatures.

I would say that we, as a species, are 'into-logic' creatures. To give us first of all the 'effect' part of 'cause and effect' works by driving us out of the logic of the story, and our powerful instinct, as Homo sapiens, is to 'turn into' it, to find our way back and understand it.

It is the favourite technique of mystery writers. To leave us out of the chain of cause-and-effect means a question is aroused in our minds — or a series of questions. We have noticed sudden alterations in our situation, a change in everyone around us, and our powerful instinct, our continual exercising of logic, compels us to find out how and why these changes happened. We must push our way back into the narrative. We can only succeed by continuing to read.

Wuthering Heights is successful, is golden, because Brontë is adept at the alchemy of fiction-writing, the spell-making, the enchantment. She conjures ingredients, and brings together or separates them, and she leans hard on her text, and she manipulates logic in order to display it in such a way as to enchant us. As a result we are given the impression of a very certain, truthful reality taking us (as willing passengers) for a ride. A profusion of specific, chosen details gives the piece its energy, and the heady language is its music. We forgive the chaos of the differing points of view and the unlikely child's diary. In the text we see and feel the truth, expressed with beauty and powerful invention and so the base metal is transformed into gold.

3. The Invasion

It is a long piece of work to write a novel, but we have started work. We have set out to cross from this side of the piece of ground, to the other.

Here is my opening for *What The Children Saw*. The siblings Emma, David and Ben, whose grandparents have all died some years ago, are waiting while their friend Megan greets all eight of *her* grandparents:

> Her grandparents arrived, set after set, and from their hideout at the bottom of the driveway the three siblings watched the last pair, numbers seven and eight, take out from the boot of their grey Mitsubishi car an Easter egg bigger than a baby. It was gaudily decorated. Megan's smile stretched from ear to ear. She held it aloft, knowing the others could see.
>
> 'Jee-sus Christ,' whispered Emma. 'Happy Easter *Megan*.'
>
> The last grandmother stooped and fastened the blue strap on her sandal.
>
> 'No-one can have eight grandparents,' said Ben.
>
> 'She can. They all got divorced and married again. So, double four, which equals eight.'
>
> 'What do you call a whole load of them together? A herd of grandparents?'
>
> 'A flock,' suggested Megan.
>
> 'Gaggle,' said Emma.

> When this last grandmother was on her way again David said of
> Megan, in a knowledgeable tone of voice, 'She told me earlier she'd
> swap all of them for a single brother or sister.'
>   'Yeah, well,' said Emma bleakly, 'she's bonkers isn't she.'

It is only the first thousand or so words, and the work stretches ahead. There are between seventy and a hundred thousand more, one by one, needing to be written. It is going to take a while.

Alongside the fun — the bliss of composition — there is a part of writing a novel that is a long trudge over the middle ground. It takes months of work.

It also demands a length of time to read a novel: a whole day, two days, three? Perhaps one might devote as much as a month's worth of free time to it. It is a protracted engagement, a lot to ask of someone. It should not feel like a slog, it must be a pleasure. We should feel compelled to read a book.

Joseph O'Neill's *Netherland* (2008) is an un-showy, deceptively simple novel and it is compelling, with passages of virtuosity. There are three strands of plot: first, a man of Dutch ancestry, Hans van den Broek, splits up with his wife and child for a year, after which they get back together. Woven into this domestic strand is a second strand, the mysterious death of a charismatic businessman who is trying to set up a cricket ground in New York State. A third, lesser strand includes patches of memory from the narrator's childhood in the Netherlands.

When I had finished reading it I felt triumphant. I had gone through this book, lived it; and to have completed it gave rise to a feeling of success, as if I had conquered this material, all the way to the end. Of course I knew it was the writer's achievement and that I was merely the passenger, but that was not how it felt. I was bound up, connected to O'Neill. He led me across that particular ground, and I succeeded thanks to him but also thanks to my commitment, my fight.

Whereas to be failed by a writer, when we throw the book across the room, or when we let it slip from nerveless fingers, or when we simply fail to pick it up again, gives rise to feelings of abandonment, of hurt, anger.

Field Marshal Sir William Slim, in his account of two military campaigns in Burma, *Defeat Into Victory* (1956), describes a troop of men left without objective, without supplies, without morale, as 'the soft skinned orange flung in front of the steamroller' (Slim, 1956: 3).

Most writers will react against being compared to an army commander, but I would ask that you bear with it. This is my third analogy: your reader is a soldier in an army of readers commanded by you, the writer. It might be a large army — a large readership — or a small, specialized force, the elite or niche sensibility of fewer readers, but in any case it is the writer's duty to lead his or her men and women and get them to the other side of the ground he or she wishes them to cover. And thereby, the writer ensures their victory. The reward this brings is described by Slim as 'the greatest unity of emotional and intellectual experience that can befall a man' (Slim, 1956: 3).

And I summon this analogy on our behalf because, as writers, we wish to avoid that self-indulgence that blights us when we stick in our own minds and write only for ourselves. This counts as dereliction of duty.

I have a room in which I write, with a grate in which I sometimes light a fire in winter-time and a table constructed out of old anchor chain welded together as the base, with the oak steps taken from a derelict monastery to make the table-top; and there is a window that looks onto a garden. A blue-tit, every spring, throws itself against the glass in a bid either to mate with its own reflection or fight with itself.

Inside the room, with its solitude and its atmosphere of inward-looking concentration, there is a danger I will behave in the same way, that I will hurl myself against my own reflection.

We must imagine an army of readers is in the room with us — hundreds of them, thousands — staring at us, waiting for instructions. Our victory will be their victory. They are dependent on us at every moment for what to do next: where to go, how to proceed. We must not 'write' so much as engineer their involvement in the story, and create their victory. And we must make it seem like it was all their own idea.

For the purposes of this analogy I will look at the personal qualities necessary for a successful army commander. He or she must have an effective voice, the tactical ability to achieve a given objective, a good control of morale, and an understanding of how to arouse and sustain feeling, including a sense of justice.

1. Voice

Joseph O'Neill describes his ambition for *Netherland* in an interview with Travis Elborough. He wanted, 'to write a novel that hinged on a voice ... It almost doesn't matter what happens or what is said, the reader just wants to remain in the company of this voice' (O'Neill 2009, p. 3 of the appendix 'About The Author').

He wanted to create a voice we would listen to, that we would find interesting in one way or another, that we would respond to, and be captivated by, and wish to follow. We need to do the same.

Does our voice have to be eloquent — should it possess powerful expressive qualities?

Field Marshal Slim recognized how different voices can work in different army commanders. He finds himself, in 1943, in Burma, serving under General Giffard, and describes the latter's voice thus: 'As a speech maker he was neither eloquent nor picturesque, but he had two things that impressed soldiers — he knew his stuff and he was dead honest. *The* quality which showed through him was integrity and that was the quality which, as much as any other, we wanted in our Army Commander' (Slim, 1956: 164).

It is worth teasing out these 'two things that impressed soldiers'. The first one is that 'he knew his stuff'. In other words, he had authority over his subject matter. The second one was ' ... *the* quality which showed through him' — integrity.

These were the two qualities which Slim believed were indispensable in the voice of an army commander: authority and integrity.

1.1. Authority

Mark Haddon wrote one of the most popular novels of the last decade, *The Curious Incident of the Dog in the Night-time* (2003). He invented as his first-person narrator a youth called Christopher, who had Asperger's Syndrome. Haddon wrote as if he himself had Asperger's.

He had the authority to do so because he was a maths genius and was mildly dysfunctional, socially, when he was young. In his earlier life he also worked in an adult training centre in North London for people with autism, observing such characters as Christopher at first hand. His creation was based on a confident interpretation of character traits well known to him. He had an intimate knowledge of the ground he wished to take us across.

It can be defined as research, and it can either be inhaled, as life experience, or sought out in books, or by interview, or in travel. It amounts to the same thing: knowledge of the ground one wishes to cover.

I can open any page of *Wolf Hall* (2009) by Hilary Mantel and find such authority. I land on page 47:

> They are taking apart the Cardinal's house. Room by room, the king's men are stripping York Place of its owner. They are bundling up parchments and scrolls, missives and memoranda and the volumes of his personal accounts; they are taking even the ink and the quills. They are prising from the walls the boards on which the cardinal's coat of arms is painted.
>
> They arrived on a Sunday: two vengeful grandees: the Duke of Norfolk a bright-eyed hawk, the Duke of Suffolk just as keen. They told the cardinal he was dismissed as Lord Chancellor, and demanded he hand over the Great Seal of England. He, Cromwell, touched the cardinal's arm. A hurried conference. The cardinal turned back to them, gracious: it appears a written request from the king is necessary; have you one? Oh: careless of you. It requires a lot of face to keep so calm; but then the cardinal has face.
>
> 'You want us to ride back to Windsor?' Charles Brandon is incredulous. 'For a piece of paper? When the situation's plain?' (Mantel, 2009: 47)

Mantel could not have lived in the sixteenth century. Yet, just as in the case of the Mark Haddon text, this quality of authority rings true in a particular way. Specifics count; but at the same time the research does not show itself as newly won. We, as readers, have ears that are finely tuned to seek out and measure authority. There is a danger in the writer trying too hard, particularly with new knowledge, which sharply reduces authority. The novelist must therefore wear his or her knowledge lightly. There is enough specific detail included here — the fact that the coats of arms are painted on boards, the use of the word 'missives', the ink and the quills — but they are apparently tossed in carelessly, so we feel her knowledge of this particular ground has been inhaled over a period of time, ingested, chewed up and spat out, rather than being freshly minted and turned out to impress us.

Our collective ear, as an army of readers, registers Mantel's authority because it strikes our ear as well worn. We therefore give her that most valuable commodity — trust. And so we follow her.

1.2. Integrity

Integrity in a voice is a more elusive quality to define. There is the notion of 'entireness, wholeness: the unimpaired state of anything' as well as 'uprightness pureness' (*Chambers Dictionary*, 1990 edn). If a person has integrity we like to think they are the same all the whole way through. They are true to themselves, and not trying to imitate anyone else.

In 1944, during the campaign to recapture Burma from the Japanese, Slim worked with a Commander Wingate, who had an unusual voice and manner. Together they oversaw a daring plan to float 65 gliders behind enemy lines so they might silently carry in the engineers, ground troops and equipment charged with preparing landing strips for the Dakotas that would ferry over the main force. In utter darkness so they would not be seen by the enemy (it was before the deployment of radar) the gliders would be towed up and let go. They were to glide behind enemy lines and land on patches of scrub cleared for the purpose by local Burmese who were on the side of the allies. This mission had been conceived by Commander Wingate, who was leading a unit they called 'Special Force'.

While they were waiting to take off, word came to them that piles of logs had been left on one of the three crude runways prepared for the gliders. Wingate was emotional, and petulant. Silences alternated with tantrums. He was not eloquent, at all. He threatened to pull out of the whole enterprise. His belief was that this could not be a co-incidence; it could only be deliberate sabotage. And then he went into a sulk and would not say a word.

The minutes ticked away. Should they abandon the mission, or carry on and bear the casualties that would inevitably come from re-directing one third of the gliders to the other two runways, where the enemy might also be waiting for them? There was a gap of ten minutes in which to decide.

They went ahead and, as it turned out, it had been a coincidence: the logs had been left there by a local tree-cutting operation. Forty-five out of the sixty-five gliders made it safely and carried in the men and materials necessary to construct, maintain and guard proper landing strips for the Dakotas that followed.

It was in one of these Dakotas that Wingate himself was killed. He 'crashed into the wild tangle of hills west of Imphal' (Slim, 1956: 268).

Slim describes Wingate's appeal to his troops thus:

> With him, contact had too often been collision, for few could meet so stark a character without being either violently attracted or re-pelled ... Without his presence to animate it, Special Force would no longer be the same to others or to itself. He had created, inspired, defended it, and given it confidence; it was the offspring of his vivid imagination and ruthless energy. (Slim, 1956: 268)

It sounds like reading Jay Griffiths, or a Ben Elton novel — he was a Marmite kind of commander. But to his followers, his voice spoke with integrity, and they followed him whatever.

Eloquence is a powerful attribute in a writer, and in an army com-mander. But it is not an essential quality, and the quest for eloquence (because it is so beguiling) often leads a writer astray. If we can achieve integrity and authority, then eloquence, on its own, will find us.

Netherland is successful in this respect. From the outset we are drawn to Hans van den Broek's voice — his straight-forward honesty about himself and about others:

The afternoon before I left London for New York — Rachel had flown out six weeks previously — I was in my cubicle at work, boxing up my possessions, when a senior vice president at the bank, an Englishman in his fifties, came to wish me well. I was surprised; he worked in another part of the building and in another department, and we were known to each other only by sight. Nevertheless, he asked me in detail about where I intended to live (Watts? Which block on Watts?) and reminisced for several minutes about his loft on Wooster Street and his outings to the 'original' Dean and DeLuca. He was doing nothing to hide his envy.

'We won't be gone for very long,' I said, playing down my good fortune. That was, in fact, the plan, conceived by my wife: to drop in on New York City for a year or three and then come back.

'You say that now,' he said. 'But New York's a very hard place to leave. And once you do leave...' The SVP, smiling, said, 'I still miss it, and I left twelve years ago.'

It was my turn to smile — in part out of embarrassment, because he'd spoken with an American openness. 'Well, we'll see,' I said.

'Yes,' he said, 'You will.'

His sureness irritated me, though principally he was pitiable — like one of those Petersburgians of yesteryear whose duties have washed him up on the wrong side of the Urals.

But it turns out he was right, in a way. (O'Neill, 2009: 1)

The integrity of the character is evident in his ability to be both critical of, and generous to, the character of the Senior Vice President, and Hans can see himself clearly, too, whether it is in a good light or a bad one. It is a quiet, understated voice, but it has integrity (and authority also, with its deft use of proper nouns).

However, there is a deliberate attempt in some fiction to create an apparent lack of authority and integrity: an unreliable narrator. On page 2 of *The Curious Incident of the Dog in the Night-time* the narrator, Christopher, reveals that he cannot understand the expressions on people's faces, other than the polar opposites of sad or happy. He admits that if someone asks him too many questions at once he cannot cope and makes 'that noise that Father calls groaning' (Haddon,

2003: 8). This narrator, surely, lacks authority. He does not know the ground as well as we do.

Mark Haddon points at the problem himself in an article in the *Observer* (Review section, 27 April 2003), 'One of the paradoxes … is that you'd think Christopher would be astonishingly ill-suited to narrate a book. He can't do metaphor, he can't understand emotions or expression, he can't see the bigger picture. He is always missing stuff'.

But what Christopher apparently lacks in authority he makes up for with the particular quality of his integrity. Within his prescribed world he has a unique brand of this valuable quality. He might miss the truth, but, like the dogs that he loves so much, he will never lie to us. And because this brand of integrity comes at us from a sideways direction, it refreshes our understanding of this principle in the human voice, and so it becomes an uncommonly powerful example of integrity, conjured in an unreliable narrator.

And there are other unexpected benefits. Mark Haddon explains, ' … ironically, once you adopt that voice, it helps you avoid a number of pitfalls that novels fall into. He never explains, he never gets in the way of his story, he never tries to make up your mind for you. He just paints a picture and leaves it to you to come to conclusions'.

It is due to the magical, gold-standard quality of Christopher's integrity that we not only forgive his lack of authority, but we work hard to provide it for him, and this demand on our attention increases our engagement with the story. The critic Kate Kellaway, who conducted the interview with Mark Haddon in the *Observer*, explains the same concept beautifully, except that she is talking about Christopher's apparent lack of emotion: ' … because Christopher's emotional repertoire does not include self-pity one rushes in after him, full of sympathy, supplying his deficiencies, doing his feeling for him, filling the void — and this makes the novel emotionally involving in an unusual way'.

There are many other examples of how novelists play fast and loose with the voice of a novel and yet manage both to secure and strengthen these two prescribed qualities of authority and integrity. We have heard enough in the previous analogy about *The Stone Diaries* by Carol Shields, but her use of an unreliable narrator is so extraordinary

---

Writing exercise no. 11: 'The right trousers'

First, to gain authority: take a section of your writing and subject each concrete noun and proper noun to an interrogation. Make a list of details (this might require research). For instance, if a vicar is giving a tea party, then take the noun 'vicar' and interrogate it. What kinds of vicar are there, and which one is he? What do they wear, how much are they paid, what are their duties. Of what is their 'vicarness' comprised? How does a dog-collar do up? Write the scene again with your new-found authority on the subject. Leave the material for a day and then read it again to see where your effort at authority has become too laboured, effortful, and then decide what to cut. This process, in addition to giving your work authority, will lead to narrative invention and other riches.

Second, to gain integrity, write a section of your novel as if you're not writing a novel at all, but instead you are writing a letter to a particular friend or relative who knows you very well, and for whom you do not have to try to be someone else.

---

that I could not resist attaching a description of the games she plays in the Appendix.

As Slim described, authority and integrity are the base notes; they are the two qualities without which a writer's voice cannot operate successfully. They create the abiding trust of those who listen, and if we trust the voice, we will follow it. On top of these two qualities, one might add that such a grip can be exerted more strongly, more luxuriously, with the use of eloquence, of musical effect (which is akin to a type of hypnotism).

What can we do to achieve such a voice? Only two things: listen carefully to writers' voices as they read themselves in our minds, and practice writing with our own voice rather than trying to achieve the voices used by others. Read and write true to our sense of things, having arrived at certain knowledge of ourselves. In other words, wear the right trousers.

In *What The Children Saw* I aim to create this kind of integrity underneath the musical effect of the voice. It is my ambition but it will take a while before I know if I have achieved it.

Megan, in her bedroom, spent a distracted ten minutes trying to put back together her model of The Human Body. It was a twelve-inch-high plastic figurine and the top of its skull lifted off so you could take out and examine its brain. An eyeball popped out and a section of the throat was removable. Its ribcage swung open to reveal all the major internal organs which fitted together like a puzzle. She dreaded losing the two kidneys, which she just knew she would, one day, but a greater problem was the liver. Once the kidneys were pressed onto their stubs near the backbone, she could replace everything else — heart, lungs, stomach — but the liver should be positioned in a particular way which she couldn't get the hang of…

When she heard the call for lunch she ditched The Human Body and went running through the house to find her grandparents returning from a tour around the garden. All of them had been married to different partners, back in time, but it was impossible now to tell who had been with whom. She could identify them as individuals even from this distance: each had a particular way of walking or standing. Grandpa Richard with his pigeon toes, Granny Annabelle with what she called her 'shufflebottom' walk, Granny Viki with her purposeful almost-trot, Granny Molly calm and good-humoured, Grandpa Eric on his sticks, Grandpa Jeremy sort of like a bear… How unusual it was, that they'd *all* visited, together.

During lunch she was anxious to escape: the clock edged closer to the time agreed for the swap — three hours with the billies in return for half an Easter egg. Being an only child and often forced, for company, to join in with grown-ups, or to wander around alone, Megan's strangely green eyes and her thoughts — and even the direction in which she habitually stood — were usually fixed on Emma's house, which was no more than a few minutes' dash through the graveyard, and, even if she was not able to visit, as many as three times a day Megan would phone. Whoever answered, Megan's first words were always the same, 'Is Emma there?' spoken in such an odd, blank voice, as if she didn't know the person who'd answered, had never gone there, whereas she spent more time in their bedrooms, in their kitchen, in their living rooms, than in her own.

After lunch, she begged her mother for permission to deliver the numerous good-byes and thank-yous to her grandparents, so she might leave.

She went to fetch the second largest Easter egg, a coruscating oval, a hollow of chocolate wrapped in gold foil, nearly as heavy as a bag of sugar, and walked out of the house. When she felt the tickle of long grass against her ankles she ran, heading for Sacred John Powell.

As she approached — the sound of her own breath loud and anxious to her own ears — she could see the hem of Emma's dress sticking out from the side of the black gravestone. 'Hi,' she said. She wished she hadn't run all the way. She should have stopped and walked the last bit.

'Hi,' said Emma. She didn't stir from her relaxed position, leaning back, one foot cocked neatly.

'Hold on,' said Megan, and she started to tear off the cardboard in order to break the egg in half.

'We agreed on the whole egg,' said Emma.

'We said half.'

'I said the whole egg, and then I said deal, and you replied — deal. So it's the whole egg.'

Megan knew she mustn't cry. If she'd had brothers and sisters of her own this would be the kind of thing she'd have to put up with, and now, if she did cry, it would be marked down as only-child behaviour. Mute, she handed it over.

Emma took the golden egg. As she turned it in her hands a glint of light was reflected skywards, like a signal, only to be seen by the birds high above, she imagined. It was like the egg had been laid by the goose from the fairy tale.

'You get rid of that,' she said and handed Megan the cardboard. And then she informed Megan where the billies could be found. 'Alderman of This Town.'

The authority of this piece depends quite heavily on using the names engraved on the headstones in a sufficiently casual manner. To begin with I had written the words, 'she declared' after Emma had given the information 'Alderman of This Town' but the addition of these two words declared only one thing: that I was pleased with my invention and wanted my readers to be impressed as well.

There are some tips we can use to help us judge the effect of our voices on our readers. First, ask someone else to read our work aloud to us — to read it aloud ourselves is a less good test. Second, print it in a different font and a different type size and then read it in a strange place — in a café or on a train — this helps us gain distance from the work, and allows us to 'hear' it as if we were the reader rather than the writer. Our task is to separate ourselves from the pleasure we take in the sound of our own voices: to become 'other'. The most effective way of doing this is to put the work away for a long time, a year, and forget about it, and then come back and read it again.

2. Objective

The skill of an Army Commander — the reason you might promote someone to such a position — is bound up with the notion of his or her *tactical* ability, which requires the ability to define clearly an appropriate objective for the campaign, and, on top of that, to have the tactical skill to achieve it.

The reader can sense the bitterness in Slim's words as he searches for the reason the 14th army was defeated in Burma in 1943. He looks back to when he first took charge, and he sees that no overall sense of objective had been made clear to them:

> It was then that we needed from the highest national authority a clear directive of what was to be our purpose in Burma. Were we to risk all in a desperate attempt to destroy the Japanese Army and recover all that had been lost? Ought we to fight to the end on some line to retain at least part of Burma? Or was our task to withdraw slowly, keeping our forces intact, while the defence of India was prepared? Had we been given any one of these as our great overall object it would have had an effect, not only on the major tactics of the campaign, but on the morale of the troops. No such directive was ever received. (Slim, 1956: 118)

They were driven out of Burma without ceremony.

The willpower, the ambition of an army commander is made concrete by the objective, on the ground. Let us say, for instance, the objective is 'to take that ridge'. It is the duty of the army commander to recruit the men and women under his or her command so that they share that ambition. Their willpower must be allied to the commander's, and so they will reach for that same objective: they become determined to take the ridge, and given the successful deployment of tactical skills, they will do so.

The writer has the same task: to recruit her or his readership, to have them follow, and keep turning the pages, and reach the top of the hill.

The army commander directly addresses his troops, and some writers on occasion directly address their readers. More commonly, though, writers of fiction address their readers via intermediaries: the characters they have created.

In Ben Rice's novella *Pobby and Dingan* the objective of the main character, Kellyanne, is strongly evident from page one:

> Kellyanne opened the car door and crawled into my bedroom. Her face was puffy and pale and fuzzed-over. She just came in and said, 'Ashmol! Pobby and Dingan are maybe dead.' That's how she said it.
>
> 'Good,' I said. 'Perhaps you'll grow up now and stop being such a fruit-loop.'
>
> Tears started sliding down her face. But I wasn't feeling any sympathy, and neither would you if you'd grown up with Pobby and Dingan.
>
> 'Pobby and Dingan aren't dead,' I said, hiding my anger in a swig from my can of Mello Yello. 'They never existed. Things that never existed can't be dead, right?'
>
> Kellyanne glared at me through tears the way she did the time I slammed the door of the ute in Dingan's face or the time I walked over to where Pobby was supposed to be sitting and punched the air and kicked the air in the head to show Kellyanne that Pobby was a figment of her imaginings. I don't know how many times I had sat at the dinner table saying, 'Mum, why do you have to set places for Pobby and Dingan? They aren't even real.' She put food out for them too. She said they were quieter and better behaved than me and deserved the grub. (Rice, 2002: 1)

Kellyanne wants her imaginary friends, Pobby and Dingan, to exist for real, to be 'found'. We arrive at a critical time: it is more than ever important for Pobby and Dingan to exist because they are lost and she thinks they are 'maybe dead.'

Kelllyanne's mother is recruited to her objective, but her brother, Ashmol, and her father, Rex, aren't. 'Me and him never took Pobby and Dingan seriously one bit' (Rice, 2002: 3) says Ashmol.

On page 2 we are introduced to the father, Rex's, ambition, *his* objective — to find an opal.

> My Dad would come back from the opal mines covered in dust, his beard like the back-end of a dog that's shat all over its tail. He would be saying, 'Ashmol, I sensed it today! Tomorrow we'll be on opal son, and we'll be bloody millionaires! I can feel those bewdies sitting there in the drives, staring back at me … there's rumours going that Lucky Jes has taken out a million-dollar stone and a fossilised mammoth tooth with a sun-flash in it. We're close, boy.' (Rice, 2002: 2)

The illusory quality of both father and daughter's desires — to find an opal and to have Pobby and Dingan actually exist — means they are inextricably bound together in our minds. His wife will, a few pages later, put it into words:

> 'Damn, Rex, You make me so bloody angry. Honestly! You haven't found any opal in two years. Not a glimpse of it. And opal's real enough for *you*. You don't stop dreaming about it and talking to it in your sleep like a lover! Well, as far as I'm concerned your bloody opal doesn't exist, either!' (Rice, 2002: 6)

Ashmol, our narrator, signs up to his father's desire to find opal, so the household is divided along gender lines: father and son are behind finding the opal, and mother and daughter are signed up to the existence of Pobby and Dingan.

We, the army of readers, are signed up to both sides. We want the boys to find the opal and we want Pobby and Dingan to exist. And we are not alone. Lightning Ridge is a town where almost everyone believes they will find an opal, and quite a few of the 'older, softer sort of folks' (Rice, 2002: 3) are willing to believe in Pobby and Dingan, too — 'every time we went to Khan's, Mrs Schwarz would hand my sister three lollies and say, "There you are, Kellyanne. One for you, one for Pobby and one for Dingan"' (Rice, 2002: 4).

I would like to coin the phrase 'a map of desire' for this orchestration of characters' willpower by the novelist. The objective of the writer is made concrete in the objectives of the character, and the rest is a question of recruitment — the recruitment of other characters in the story (or losing their support) and the recruitment of the reader, either to share in what that particular character wants, and to want it for them, or the opposite. Either way, the sense of willpower engaged, the sense of ambition, creates momentum, traction in the story, towards the objective. We will work hard to get to the top of the ridge, fighting alongside our characters, or we will watch from a distance, through binoculars, spellbound and horrified, as they struggle to the top of the ridge where we know an ambush is waiting for them. Either way, it is a tactical ability in the writer that is demanded, if the sense of objective is to be engaged.

On page 7, following his wife's outburst, Rex apparently switches sides and suddenly believes in Pobby and Dingan. As his son, Ashmol, reports:

> Well, after my mum said this stuff about opal and after she'd done her usual piece about there being no money left in the tin under the bed, Dad sulked around a bit and kicked a few rocks around out in the yard. But then suddenly the door swung open and he came in full of energy like a new man and with a strange smile on his face. And what did he do? He started asking Kellyanne about Pobby and Dingan and how their days had been and what they were doing tomorrow. And he had never done that before in his life, ever. But he did it in a voice so you weren't too sure if he was joking around or not. Kellyanne was studying his face carefully, trying to work him out for herself. And so was I. And so was Mum. (Rice, 2002: 7)

Ben Rice's army of readers are standing shoulder to shoulder with Kellyanne: our willpower is attached to hers, we're moving in the same direction. We are hoping to cover the ground and achieve the existence of Pobby and Dingan. Now we have apparently been joined by Rex, her Dad, and even though we are not sure of his motives, we sense that if he really is joining us, it will intensify our desire, both on behalf of the character of Kellyanne and on our own account, to bring

Pobby and Dingan into existence. The ridge is within sight and we are climbing.

Rex is up to something, however. He takes Pobby and Dingan for rides in the ute — 'Sorry, son. Can't take you today, Ashmol. Not enough room with Pobby and Dingan in here' (Rice, 2002: 8) — and he helps them get dressed and so on. But we know he is just pretending, in order to keep his wife off his back about the opals.

This leads to the crisis that opens the story. Rex offers to take Pobby and Dingan out to the opal mine so they can get some exercise while Kellyanne's at school, and Kellyanne agrees. But when Rex returns, he has forgotten about Pobby and Dingan. Kellyanne asks him, 'Dad. Where's Pobby and Dingan? Where are they?' Rex is thrown for a moment, he goes red in the face, but he quickly recovers. 'Relax now, darl. Pobby and Dingan's right here sittin' on the couch next to Ashmol' (Rice, 2002: 10).

It was the wrong thing to have said, and Kellyanne has seen through him. '"No they're not, Dad," she said. "They hate Ashmol. Where are they really?"' (Rice, 2002: 10).

Rex tries to recover, and gives several more answers as to where Pobby and Dingan might be, but nothing works. They have to head out to the claim, in the dark, to hunt for Pobby and Dingan. Rex even looks in the next door claim, a mine belonging to Old Sid the Grouch. The latter appears from his tin shack and accuses Rex of 'ratting' on his claim. The police are called and Rex is arrested and spends the night in jail. Worse, some other miners hear that Rex was ratting on Sid's claim and set the fence alight and paint insults on the wall.

Suddenly, things are serious. Pobby and Dingan are lost and 'maybe dead'. And we get the first hint, now, of Ashmol's recruitment to Kellyanne's objective — 'But I was half thinking of Dad and if he was in prison and how the whole thing was Pobby and Dingan's fault. And then I tried to get my head round how it could be their fault if they didn't even exist. And I fell asleep thinking about that' (Rice, 2002: 18).

Kellyanne falls sick because 'she was very tired and worried because Pobby and Dingan hadn't come back, and that she couldn't be sure if they were dead or not' (Rice, 2002: 22).

Ashmol thinks Kellyanne is 'faking at first, pretending to be ill like she pretended to have friends. But then I heard her puking up in the dunny. She *was* sick' (Rice, 2002: 22).

This leads to the first stage in Ashmol's recruitment. He does not exactly believe in Pobby and Dingan's existence, but he signs up to the idea of 'finding' them. His family is in real trouble, with a court case hanging over his father and his sister refusing to eat. He wants 'the Williamson family name to gleam and sparkle and be all right' (Rice, 2002: 25). The only way he can think of to do this is to tell everyone in the whole town they have to find Pobby and Dingan. 'I stayed awake all the bastard-night trying to get my head around the problem' (Rice, 2002: 25).

What grips about the scenario now is the two opposite ways in which brother and sister go about achieving the same objective. Kellyanne is passive-aggressive. She does less and less. She stays in bed and only becomes more ill. Ashmol's willpower, as a consequence of this, heads in the other direction: he visits every bar in town, and the Wallangalla Motel, and the bowling club. He interrupts the poker players, and tells everyone what's happened to his sister and that her imaginary friends Pobby and Dingan need to be found. He breaks into the line-dancing:

> I tried to go up to people on the dance floor and get them to stop dancing and listen, but they were too busy doing their moves ... In the end I just walked up to the bloke with the tape decks and grabbed the microphone and shouted, 'Ladies and gents! Sorry to interrupt your dancing, but my name's Ashmol Williamson, and my sister is sick and we need to help her find her imaginary friends tomorrow morning!' (Rice, 2002: 27)

Kellyanne's sickness now adds to the desire both in us and in the characters to reach the objective — to find Pobby and Dingan. This intensification of the desire is the reason we cannot wait to turn the page. It provides forward momentum to the story. The willpower of Kellyanne is now added to the willpower of Ashmol, and to our willpower, to an increasing extent.

The empathy we feel for this little boy — doing all he can to mend his family — adds to the intensity of our willpower engaged on his behalf. Look at the signs he puts up all round the place:

LOST! HELP!

KEILLYANNE WILLIAMSON'S FRIENDS POBBY AND DIN-GAN.

DESCRIPTION: IMAGINARY, QUIET.

REWARD IF FOUND (Rice, 2002: 32)

It breaks your heart. Everything — character, humour, righteousness — is pouring into the story to support this objective. Everything hangs on it: his sister's life, his parents' marriage, the court case. We really are climbing for that ridge, hand over feet.

The recruitment-drive intensifies when a certain number among the townsfolk make it plain they also are looking for Pobby and Dingan. Kellyanne is lifted from her sickbed and taken for a drive in the ute so she can see the signs and watch people searching. 'I saw some of the line-dancers had a banner saying *Pobby and Dingan search party*' (Rice, 2002: 36). The search for the imaginary friends is attached more strongly to the search for opal in the mines when Kellyanne reveals that, 'Dingan had a lovely opal in her belly-button, only you had to be a certain kind of person to see it' (Rice, 2002: 35).

None of it works: the family is disintegrating. Kellyanne is losing weight. The father leaves home in the middle of the night.

A succession of townsfolk turn up saying they have found Pobby and Dingan but of course they have not, not really. Kellyanne sees through their attempts to fool her. She makes an appeal to her brother: he must go and look down the opal mine, because she has a hunch they are down there, still. 'And go alone and at night so people won't be able to see you' (Rice, 2002: 48).

He complains that even if he does go, he will not be able to see them, not like she can. Kellyanne does not answer. 'She had fallen asleep, and her arms were thin and deathly-looking. There were rings under her eyes and her face was the colour of shin-cracker' (Rice, 2002: 48).

This leads to Ashmol's final, complete recruitment and to the achievement of the objective. He goes alone, at night, down the mine. He knows these drives well and unwinds his string to follow his torch down. He finds a spill of earth from a section of the roof that's collapsed. 'I said to myself, "What if Pobby and Dingan got caught under the pile of rock?" And then I listened carefully and sort of convinced myself that I could hear a little moaning and breathing' (Rice 2002: 54).

He begins to pull off the stones, and underneath he finds 'the wrapper of a Violet Crumble chocolate bar' (Rice, 2002: 54). This was Pobby and Dingan's favourite food. 'But then suddenly my eye caught hold of something else flashing up at me. Something sitting there in the dark. Waiting. A sort of greeny-red glint ... my heart beat the world record for the pole vault ... I licked the nobbie ... It was opal. Green. Red. Black. All of them together' (Rice, 2002: 55). For real, he has found an opal. A huge one. As he contemplates what has happened, he realizes, 'Shit, we Williamsons are going to be rich bastards' (Rice, 2002: 55).

But his ambition for the opal is corrupted, cross-fertilized, by his desire for Pobby and Dingan to exist and therefore his sister to be saved. He looks at the opal and realizes that, 'This is Dingan's belly button' (Rice, 2002: 55). To find the opal is to find Pobby and Dingan; they are the same thing. And as he leaves the mine, 'At the foot of the ladder I paused and set Pobby and Dingan down gently, remembering that there was no way a little bloke like me was going to get them up to the top all by myself' (Rice, 2002: 56).

We are at the top of the ridge and Ben Rice used all his technical skill, coupled to the willpower of his characters, to drive us up here. We believe in Pobby and Dingan. And the height to which we have been lifted is secured, made safe, suddenly, when Kellyanne believes that yes, Pobby and Dingan are dead. She then goes on to remind Ashmol that Dingan always said the opal in her belly button must be used to pay for the funeral, when she dies. Kellyanne makes Ashmol promise not to make money out of the opal, not to tell anyone about it, except the funeral director. 'This is Dingan's bellybutton. This isn't some ordinary stone you can go making a heap of money from' (Rice, 2002: 60).

Ashmol has to make a choice: to sell the opal and make a million dollars, or stick with his belief in Pobby and Dingan and save his sister's life. 'I thought about this long and hard, and I thought what a shame it was that I was going to be giving away my first red on black. And then I said, "I promise not to go making any money on it." And then I left the room, almost worn out with promising"' (Rice, 2002: 60).

The whole town turns up to the funeral of a child's imaginary friend. The poignancy and the emotional impact of this invention, with all of Ashmol's generosity and willpower pushing against it, is intensely moving. Ben Rice has created our belief in fictional characters, who themselves create belief in the two fictional characters, Pobby and Dingan.

Such a simple, strong delivery of a clearly defined objective is particularly evident in successful novels commanding a large army of readers. For instance, to return to a previous example, it is significant how Mark Haddon and his narrator, Christopher, define for us the objective so early in *The Curious Incident of the Dog in the Night-time*. It comes on page one. Christopher finds a dog named Wellington dead on his neighbour's lawn, with a fork driven through it. He says, 'I stroked Wellington and wondered who had killed him, and why' (Haddon, 2003: 1). The aim of this campaign, this book, is clear. On page 5, they — Mark Haddon and Christopher together — give a typically straightforward account of their shared objective: 'So I am writing a murder-mystery novel' (Haddon, 2003: 5).

Mark Haddon commands a large, broad-based readership, high and low brow, children and adults alike. He is aware of the importance of creating early on in his readers a sense of what the overall objective is and not only creating it, but recruiting his army to join in with that objective, and, during the campaign, reinforcing their commitment to the objective.

Joseph O' Neill, a novelist with a more specialized, literary readership, makes use of a similar technique. On page 3 his dead body turns up, described in a phone call the narrator receives out of the blue from a journalist — 'She tells me that Chuck's "remains" have been found in the Gowanus canal' (O'Neill, 2009: 4). The narrator, Hans, replies 'You have quite a story on your hands' (O'Neill, 2009: 4).

O'Neill oscillates back and forth in time in order to create intrigue in his display of logic, whereas Mark Haddon walks his narrator forwards in time in a more simple progression. O'Neill's objective is not stated in such a bald way as Mark Haddon's; nonetheless it is the ridge that is put in front of us and our curiosity compels us to climb it. We want to find out what happened to Chuck that he comes to be lying at the bottom of the canal, murdered.

I described this way of creating an objective — by jumping back and forth in time — in the previous analogy, The Alchemist. It depends on our delight in cause-and-effect, in logic, to arouse our curiosity when either the cause or the effect is left out.

Whether you look at the technique as a manipulation of our delight in logic, or as a tactic used by writers (especially mystery writers, and those with literary readerships) to create an objective for their army of readers, is immaterial; the result is the same: there is forward progression towards the objective, the march on the ridge.

It is a tactic that is used copiously in O'Neill's *Netherland*. A striking example is found on page 180. We have been trained from the outset of this novel to leap adroitly back and forth in time, and when Hans van den Broek, the narrator, hears his wife call up to him from downstairs, 'Tea?' O'Neill uses the sound of her voice, calling this exact same question, 'Tea?' in order to take us back to a scene that happened three years previously:

> I actually flinch. It comes to me, this question, as the pure echo of an identical offer she voiced three years ago.
> 'Tea?' Rachel asked.
> This was in London, in her parents' kitchen. I sat at the dining table with my son and his grandparents. Yes, please, I called back, gratified and a little puzzled by her kindliness.
> For during the first week of that summer holiday — this was in early August 2003 — Rachel had been in a polite mood. She was considerate and attentive and low-key and, like her parents, powerfully exer-

cised by my preferences. Everybody was making an effort for Hans: and unwarrantedly and (in retrospect) suspiciously so, because, as previously noted, I'd been an absentee for much of that summer.

The tea was poured. I engaged Jake in conversation.

'Who's your best friend at camp?' I said. 'Cato?' I had heard all about Cato. I imagined him grave and severe, like Cato Uticensis.

Jake shook his head. 'Martin is my friend.'

'Right,' I said. This was a new name. 'Does Martin like Gordon The Express? How about Diesel?'

My son nodded emphatically. 'Well, that's good,' I said. 'He sounds like a very nice boy.' I looked at Rachel. 'Martin?'

She sprang from her chair in tears and ran up the stairs. I had no idea what was happening. 'You'd better go up,' Mrs Bolton told me, exchanging furious glances with her husband.

My wife was lying face down on her bed.

'I'm sorry,' she said. 'I should have told you. That was awful. I'm sorry'. (O'Neill, 2009: 180)

We learn that 'Martin' is not a child but an adult, and the man with whom Rachel's had an affair. Even within the detail of the scene, we create a mini-objective by putting Rachel's reaction in front of us: the effect — her jumping up in tears and running off — before the cause, which is our understanding that she is having an affair. But the larger objective is also in place: we are observing this scene from a future time, when they are happily together again, so what went wrong with the affair, or what went right with the marriage, to bring us to this point — here? The objective is determined: this mending or partial mending of a marriage, at the same time as our curiosity is aroused — how did it happen? — to make sure we want to get here.

It is a tactic that has an equivalent in the theatre of war. Field Marshal Slim calls it 'the hook'. It was used by the Japanese when driving the allies out of Burma in 1943.

During their defeat, Slim had been caught out by 'the hook'. The only way to travel in Burma, they believed, was down the narrow roads that followed the rivers at the bottom of the steep-sided valleys. The sides were impenetrable, covered with dense jungle. The Japanese, however, knew better. Faced with the armoured columns advancing towards them down these tracks, the Japanese would melt into the jungle and loop around, and insert themselves some distance ahead. A simple road block would cut off supplies to the advance guard, who were then easy to pick off.

They leapt a certain distance ahead, and then turned their attention on the enclosed space, and filled it with gunfire.

They deployed this 'hook' technique again and again, eating up the allies' men and munitions, without much loss to their own side. By the time the allies had come to their senses, it was too late. The allies thought the jungle was impenetrable and that the ridges between the valleys could not be traversed; the Japanese knew the ground; their success in general-ship was because 'they had a perfect instrument for the type of operation they intended' and 'their use of it was unhesitating and accurate' (Slim, 1956: 118).

The hook is everywhere, especially in literary fiction. In Jane Feaver's collection of short stories, *Love Me Tender,* not just one but two dead bodies turn up at the start of the story 'Dancing On A Pin'. First of all Dennis ('The only way they knew it were him at the start, that oilskin, melted in the glass like butter — in a pool' [Feaver, 2009: 3]) and also Irene ('What there was left of her (some had it down to fillings and the studs of her earrings)' [Feaver, 2009: 3]). We make it our objective to find out what happened. To do so we have to press on.

Carol Shields uses it continuously in *The Stone Diaries* and I have included a description of how she does so in the Appendix.

We must think about this question of objective — because it is not absolutely necessary; there are plenty of great books which are not page-turners, and do not engage with this sense of objective. However, if there is not one, we must be sure there are other pleasures with which to enchant the reader and thereby maintain their loyalty to our text: perhaps our observational prowess, our poetic description, the new insight we might offer, our sense of humour.

In *13 Ways of Looking at the Novel* (2005), Jane Smiley defines such pleasures for us:

> The novelist has many pleasures to offer — the unusual pleasure of the exotic, the intellectual pleasure of historical understanding, the

humane pleasure of psychological insight into one or more characters, the simple pleasure of entertainment and suspense, the exuberant pleasure of laughter and trickery, the guilty pleasure of gossip, the tempting pleasure of secrecy and intimacy, the confessional pleasure of acknowledged sin and attempted redemption, the polemical pleasure of indignation, the rigorous pleasure of intellectual analysis, the reassuring pleasure of identification with one's nation or people, and the vicarious pleasure of romance. (Smiley, 2006: 86)

A significant number of modernist and post-modern writers will rush to deliver these pleasures, and, to the extent they can, avoid engaging with plot; they kick against plot, against this mimesis or manipulation, for the same reason that readers kick against it: because it is difficult to do, and for the most part it is done badly.

The examples I have used all concern themselves with the deaths of various characters, but, in the first section of *What The Children Saw*, I have my objective clearly in mind: the ridge I aim to reach is the resurrection, the bringing back to life, of Muddy Grandpa. A grandparent for the Gough siblings. In the spirit of Easter, he is going to be brought back from the dead.

It is Megan who wants it for them: she feels that it is an injustice, that she has eight Easter eggs while they have none. Her friends should have a grandparent of their own.

If Megan is the vessel I have chosen to carry this desire, then it is the unfairness of the situation that is the wind in her sails. I want to talk about right and wrong later on; suffice to say that morality, a sense of right and wrong, is part of the fabric of story.

I have worked out how to get us there, and I wrote it out, but found it was too long to include here as an extract. And then, when I was rewriting this, I thought that I should shorten it by writing it as a stage play. If Joyce, if David Lodge can suddenly include dramatic text within other forms, then so might I. Written as a stage play, with only dialogue and the action in note form, the extract is half the length, but still much too long.

It remains for me to step sideways for a while into a separate book, *What The Children Saw*, to try it out.

Living room of Emma, David and Ben's family home. Megan marches in purposefully, followed by David and Ben. She has got them for three hours on their own.

Megan puts her hand in the sideboard cupboard (like she imagined earlier) and lifts out four funeral urns. She lines them up on the floor.

David and Ben talk in hushed voices.

Ben: We can't!

Megan: But. We have to be able to see them properly. Don't we.

David: We were told never to touch...

Megan: (interrupts) *You* were told, yes. Now, which one?

Ben: I'm not sure which is which.

Ben kneels to look closer at the funeral urns.

Emma is hidden somewhere, observing, while finishing Megan's medium-sized Easter egg. She has chocolate all round her mouth. She's no sooner there, than she's gone again.

Ben reads out the names on the urns.

Ben: Grey Granny, Granny Brown. Yellow...

Megan: Were all your grandparents named after colours?

David: No ... here. Muddy Grandpa. He was ...

Ben: Hold on, listen.

They stop dead. Sound of footsteps.

Ben: Shall I put them back?

They hear the sound of their mother's voice.

Mother: IN THE BLOODY UTILITY ROOM!

They freeze. Then silently begin to put the urns back.

They listen as the footsteps turn the other way, diminish… there are still two urns left.

Megan: Ben, choose one.

David: Not Muddy Grandpa.

Megan: Why not Muddy Grandpa?

David: He was depressed. He was always sick. We don't want Muddy Grandpa.

Ben: Life's not all Oooh la la, you know.

Megan: What about Granny Green.

David: Green Granny was the most fun.

Ben: All right.

David: Amazing picnics.

Megan: Put the other one back.

Ben: She won't be able to buy us an egg.

Megan: Who says?

Ben: Hel*lo*… she won't have any money. She's been dead for flipping years.

Megan: Shh!!

They hear more noises — grown-ups' voices coming closer.

Mother: I DON'T KNOW. JUST PUT IT AWAY.

Father: I will put it away darling, right now.

Mother: HONESTLY SOMETIMES IT'S LIKE I HAVE FOUR CHILDREN, NOT THREE

Ben struggles to pick up an urn, put it back on the shelf.

Father: All right darling.

Mother: You'd think I wouldn't have to say the same thing over and over again to …

Ben looks uncertain about which urn he's put back. He's checking the labels.

Megan: Just bring it!

David: Ben, leave it!

Ben puts it back, picks it up and staggers off after them, carrying the one containing Muddy Grandpa's ashes, and follows them.

Mother: … to a grown up man with a pair of big flapping ears either side of his great lummox of a face.

Father: Ok, my sweetness. Just doing it now my love.

Move with the children to their den in the garden. A hidden spot, away from the house.

Megan, David and Ben crawl in. The urn is carried by Ben. A big bottle of water is carried by Megan. Ben puts the urn on the tree trunk. They gather round.

David: Ben, you can't really believe her.

Ben   What d'you mean?

Megan: Don't worry Ben. Your elder brother is just scared.

David: You can't really bring someone back to life.

Ben: Are you tricking me?

Megan: No. We all learnt about it in school. You did too.

David: Learnt about what at school?

Megan: David is more scared than you are, Ben.

Ben: That the human body is 99 per cent water.

Megan: Exactly. Go on, take off the lid.

David: You know, those really are Muddy Grandpa's ashes, for real. You can't turn them into mush.

Megan: This is for real. This isn't a game. The human body is ninety-nine per cent water.

Megan: You brought the wrong urn, Ben. This is Muddy Grandpa.

Ben: Doesn't matter.

David: You did that on purpose.

Ben: What's wrong with that?

Megan unscrews the top from the water bottle. Emma (unseen by them) observes from some distance away.

Megan: Stand back. Go on, Ben.

David: Don't.

Megan: Dare you.

David: Don't, Ben.

Megan: I dare you I dare you I dare you I dare you …

Ben pours water onto the ashes.

David: Christ! We are in such big time doolally trouble.

Ben: Will he be really old?

Megan: He will be exactly like he was when he died.

David: Megan. For God's sake.

Megan: There has to be enough water. Otherwise he won't grow properly.

Megan pours on more water.

David: Ben, you do know, don't you, that this isn't going to happen. It's a trick.

They stare. Nothing happens.

Megan: I think you have to poke it.

Megan hands Ben a stick.

David: It's cruel to trick him.

Megan: Go on.

Ben: Are you tricking me?

Megan: Watch out. It might kick off really quickly.

Ben summons up the courage to prod the water-and-ashes mixture.

Megan: Anything?

Ben: Not yet.

David: Oh, a bit more water, Ben; that will do it.

Megan offers her water bottle, to help Ben.

Megan: Yes it will actually, good idea.

David: Don't be such goof balls.

They wait. Nothing.

Ben: *Is* it a trick?

David: It's a game.

Ben: *Is* it?

Megan: It's a good game.

Ben: A game.

Megan: Yes.

Ben: (suddenly tearful) You *idiot*!

Ben storms off.

Emma: You'd better say sorry.

Megan: Sorry Ben!

David: I did warn you …

Megan: Ben, come back!

David: I'll go and get him.

David goes after Ben. After a while, Megan follows.

The urn is left there. Silence. After a while, there comes a plop and a low, hissing noise. Sounds of the children playing happily in the distance. The hissing is louder, and there are pluppps and fffthts and a sppluddd … Then it stops.

The children tear through, in the middle of a different game. Emma is playing as well by now.

Megan: That's not fair!

David: Is!

Ben: You didn't actually touch the base.

David: I kicked it.

Emma: I saw it, he did …

They've gone.

The hissing is louder … then stops again. Then, an enormous gurgle. Like an indoor firework, a figure grows from the urn — Muddy Grandpa. But he's not all there — he's a skeleton partially covered in flesh and skin, with a hinged ribcage behind which can be seen his vital organs — heart pumping, liver, kidneys etc. — a life-size, moving version of Megan's human body toy.

Muddy Grandpa is brought to life. I tried to create the sense of objective in the reader by leaping ahead in time and by deliberately not explaining what the game is — to add the water to the ashes — and so the reader is asked to catch up. I have attempted to attach a

---

Writing exercise no. 12: 'The map of desire'

Think of an objective for your character — let's say, for instance, that an eleven-year-old girl is going to run away from home. This is the point to which you must bring not only your character, but your readers.

Decide whether or not she wants to run away from home, or maybe she doesn't want to run away, but is going to have to. Arrange the psychology of the situation.

Now draw a 'map of desire' describing how you are going to get your readers to the same point. Are your readers going to be carried along by the character's rightful desire to run away, or are they going to swept along by dread, that the character must on no account run away, but is going to, anyway? Or are you going to create a 'hook', a gap in the logic, by going back and forth in time and therefore arousing in us sufficient curiosity, so we ask the question, 'Why did she leave home?' and therefore we are compelled to find out? Once you have done it one way, try it another way. And once you have done it for one incident, try it for another.

Your question will remain the same: how do I get my readers where I want them to be?

---

slender moral force to the objective: it is only right that a girl with eight grandparents, and therefore eight Easter eggs, should help her friends to have a grandparent of their own. I know that *I* have climbed the ridge — I can see for miles. But, have I carried my readers with me? An army commander can look over his shoulder and check that his troops are following, whereas I have to know in advance that they *will* be following. What must we do, to feel in our bones that we have got our readers with us?

An editor or an agent is available to some of us. It is a good idea to invite another writer to read it, and see what the result is.

I hope I have succeeded. There is a terrible cost, in terms of work and effort, if I have not. Field Marshal Slim writes of his pain as he was defeated in Burma in 1943. Their final task before leaving Burma was to blow the Axa Bridge. 'With a resounding thump it was blown at 2359 hours on 30th April, and its centre spans fell neatly into the river — a sad sight, and a signal that we had lost Burma' (Slim, 1956: 88).

The allies withdrew behind the Indian border and licked their wounds. Their morale had been destroyed.

3. Morale

Field Marshal Slim describes this unequivocally: 'The most important thing about a commander is his effect on morale' (Slim, 1956: 36). It is a responsibility which is attached equally strongly to the writer of fiction. If the reader's morale is high, they will want to carry on.

Slim divided morale into three areas. He said, 'Morale depends on so many things: spiritual, intellectual, and material' (Slim, 1956: 36). I want to borrow this classification.

A soldier's *material* requirements, if one is to maintain his morale, are food and drink, as well as sufficient rest and relaxation, and the equipment and the training necessary to fulfil the task that is asked of him.

First among the *intellectual* requirements, I would propose, is the sense of purpose, the aiming at an objective, that I have just explored. Beyond this overriding concern I would also place into this category the control that the army commander must exert over the feelings aroused in the mind of our soldier — a love of his or her country, a hatred of the enemy, a sense of excitement in the execution of the mission, as well as fear of failure, and perhaps a sense of humour in the face of adversity, as well, properly, as feelings of pity, and mercy, for one's opponents. Because, in the end, it is these feelings that define — and are defined by — our intellectual judgements and, in turn, they prompt our most committed actions. The army commander must therefore understand human emotions and know how they work, how to evoke and control them.

The *spiritual* requirements, I would suggest, equate to belief — which is born out of righteousness. The word morale is contained within the word morality, and perhaps there is no more powerful component within morale than this spiritual requirement, that one's sense of right and wrong is being answered. One can go without food and drink, without rest and relaxation, one can be numb, without feeling, one can lack an objective and still not give up, but without a sense that one fights on the side of righteousness a soldier's will to carry on is deflated. It is a highly individual matter: the mercenary soldier, for instance, will think it is right enough that he has been paid. But morale will be evident to the highest degree in the revolutionary soldier who believes he or she has an enormous weight of justice on her side. This sense of right and wrong is the bedrock from which will spring the impetus for this invasion. Even in our defeat, maybe especially in our defeat, we must be convinced of the righteousness of our cause. Others might not agree with us, we might even see clearly and admit the crimes we ourselves commit as soldiers — the cruelties we perpetrate on others — but if we are convinced of the overall righteousness of what we do, we will fight on.

That is all very well for soldiers, but how does a writer answer his readers' material, intellectual and spiritual needs?

3.1. Material needs

The material needs — the food and drink - for a reader, I would argue, are words, sentences and paragraphs, composed in a series of pictures to enchant the mind's eye and in a series of songs to enchant the ear. The novelist Francine Prose describes it perfectly in *Reading Like A Writer* (2006), when she remembers her childhood: 'Reading was like eating alone, with that same element of bingeing' (Prose, 2006: 7). She goes on to describe how choice of words, sentences and paragraphs sustains a reader. 'All the elements of good writing depend on the writer's skill in choosing one word instead of another' (Prose, 2006: 16). Many creative writing handbooks and classes concentrate on this subject. Earlier this morning (20 November 2010) I opened the Review section of the *Guardian* to find (on page 5) Maggie O'Farrell's tribute to the poet Michael Donaghy, 'He taught me ... that every word must pull its weight, never to use abstracts ... he said to avoid the construct ... cut it, quick, before anyone sees it'. The most sustaining words are concrete nouns, the most energy-giving are verbs. The trickiest to swallow are adjectives and adverbs. On these matters of 'food and drink', the writers Francine Prose, David Lodge, Jane Smiley, George Orwell, Eudora Welty, and Janet Burroway and Elizabeth Stuckey-French have all written works of great insight and technical knowledge and I have included them in an appendix which suggests some further reading.

An important material need, also, is described by the acronym R and R — army slang for rest and recuperation. Carol Shields accepts that excitement can become wearisome, conflict can become stale, and drama can become inert, and seeks to replace them often enough with calmness, or observation, or lack of 'scene' or incident. In *The Stone Diaries*, in the section titled '*Sorrow, 1965*', Shields suddenly composes a series of short sections from multiple points of view, giving everyone's theory as to why the narrator, Mrs Flett, 'fell into a profound depression' (Shields, 1993/2008: 229). The use of all these different, other voices (each short section titled '*Joan's Theory*' or '*Freddy Hoyt's Theory*', etc.) is refreshing because for a while we listen to voices that are different from the voice of the narrator. Similarly, on pages 49–55, Shields uses letters to the same effect. The canvas is broadened out, away from the claustrophobic, intimate birth scene, to larger horizons, in terms of geography and in terms of the enlargement of the cast of characters. During the family portrait which is described in the section titled *Motherhood*, from page 157–96, we change from one character's point of view to another's, and from background painting to detailed portrait, from interior landscape to exterior. Likewise refreshment and rest is also available by changing the modes of telling from dialogue, to action, to habitual action, to description, to letters, to the local newspaper's social column, and the gardening column.

In short, Carol Shields mixes it up. She senses when there has been enough of one thing, and changes us to a different thing. In this way she keeps her readers' responses fresh during the very long engagement that is the reading of a novel. In *Experience* (2000), Martin Amis describes how his father advised him never to use the same word to commence two paragraphs appearing within sight of each other.

Furthermore, a material requirement for our reader is training. It is important to the success of *Netherland* that from the outset Joseph O'Neill trains us to leap from one year to another. All the narrative devices: the false perspectives, the tricks with time, the affair and the revealing of the affair, require us to be adept at jumping back and forth and he begins to train us to do this immediately. In the first few paragraphs of the book (I quoted them earlier), both the characters leap back and forth to the edges of the novel's timeframe, plus that sentence is thrown in, in parenthesis, 'Rachel had flown out six weeks earlier' (O'Neill 2009, 1). We become fit and agile, able easily to skip months, or years, and then back.

So much for the material requirements of our reader.

3.2. Intellectual needs

The second category of need on which morale depends — the intellectual needs — we have gone into to some extent. A sense of purpose, the desire to achieve an objective, is perhaps the single most important intellectual requirement of a reader.

However, an additional intellectual demand is that readers should have their feelings engaged in a satisfactory way. We live our lives, for the most part, indulging in a complicated relationship with emotion. At their best our feelings are what make life worth living; at their worst, unhappiness looms. In any case, they are costly and can lead to suffering. The bliss associated with love is dangerous because that love might be taken away, or it might lead us over the edge of a cliff, or it might atrophy and die and the loss assaults us slowly. Anger and aggression might cost us dear. Excitement can have grave penalties in reality because it is attached to risk. Part of the reason we open the pages of a novel is to enjoy vicariously the excitement of having our feelings exercised without having to suffer the penalties. When all is read and done the emotions were not real: neither the danger was real, nor the grief; the love was not real either. We close up the book between its covers and escape scot-free.

And perhaps this analogy has to bulge at the sides a bit here, because of the importance of this subject. An army commander has a given set of circumstances to deal with, and must always arouse the same feelings (courage, optimism, belief, patriotism) whereas the novelist has an infinite variety of circumstances in front of her, which she has to invent, organize and confabulate, and she has every colour of feelings to deal in. It is the task of the writer to understand and portray the workings of human emotions, and furthermore he or she might want to arouse them, also. A writer might wish to create excitement, inspire love, or instil fear.

For this reason — the bulge in the analogy — I will take my time to explore this subject, and it might be that we wander a little way off from Field Marshal Slim for a while.

To re-cap: it is the task of the novelist not only to awaken but to captivate his readers both in their minds and bodies, to invade and to command their loyalty, hold them enthralled for a substantial number of hours, and there is no more powerful way of doing so than by evoking in them an emotional response — to arouse and entertain their feelings.

To investigate how we might do this, I propose to take just one soldier from among the army, and I will invite him (man or woman) to put down his weapons, un-shoulder his pack, take off his boots, and lie down on a table in front of me, so I can examine him, identify his feelings, look at how they work.

Feelings — such a spidery word — creep up on us. I will state the obvious just to emphasize that they are physical, concrete: feelings are seated in different parts of the body, and are triggered by heavily used, automatic reactions such as sexual desire, the instinct to fight, or take flight. The extent to which they are engaged is controlled by secretions like adrenaline and endorphins — physical processes.

They are key to our survival, to our happiness, but for the most part remain if not dormant then subdued in our everyday life. Often they must be forcibly subdued, for safety's sake. Yet they roil beneath the surface like dangerous subterranean seas.

3.2.1. Excitement

All forms of story-telling can be defined as acts of mimesis, and this type of mimicry (the type that seeks to arouse feelings) does not look so much for voice or manner , but instead looks for the shapes of life's events that create feeling.

Excitement, let us say, is a feeling which is created by the release of adrenaline into the blood. Located just above our volunteer reader's kidneys are the twin adrenal glands, part of the endocrine system. The core of the adrenal gland is the glamorously named Medulla, and she is the one who produces *catecholamines adrenaline* and *noradrenaline*, the water-soluble hormones that create our fight-or-flight system. And to a large extent these two hormones are excited by the same circumstances in all of us. The writer's task is to recognize the forms in real life that create these stimuli, and to lift them across from real life and use them (gracefully) in his or her fiction.

Children are reservoirs of feeling and every parent will recognize this scenario: three bored children drag their feet on the walk up to the top of the ridge. To create excitement, we either suggest we are a monster and we are going to chase them, or we propose they race each other to the top. Suddenly they will run, and not only that, they will enjoy intense excitement at the prospect of winning, and pleasure at having won.

The notion of the chase and / or race is a staple construct in those many stories that intend to provoke excitement. To chase after someone is to excite both the chased and the chaser. There are other shapes to be made use of: secrets are exciting, for instance, and also, to be in suspense is to be dangled in a state of dreadful excitement.

There is no more compelling and gruesome arena in which these particular shapes are borrowed and used mercilessly than in reality TV shows like *Big Brother* and *I'm A Celebrity Get Me Out Of Here*. The intense boredom of the contestants' lives in *Big Brother* is relieved by daily competitions and races, with serious penalties attached to winning or losing. They are playing for food and drink. If they lose they are on hunger-making rations. More compelling still are when the daily competitions and races are attached to moral judgements. In *Big Brother 5* a steel grid was lowered that cut the house in half. One side was the rich side, with good food and other treats. The other side was the poor side, with little food, no treats, few toiletries, even. Every week the rich side had to vote one person across to the poor side, while the poor side had to vote one of their number to be elevated to the rich side. The complicated patterns of right and wrong — in the race either to remain in, or go to, the rich side — made it a toe-curling study of human character.

In real life, adrenaline junkies will go to extreme lengths to provoke the drug into entering their bloodstreams: leaping from an aeroplane, bungee jumping, riding on a rollercoaster with its fast switches and turns, its ups and downs, its massive acceleration and deceleration. Writers who wish to generate excitement will borrow from such phenomena, because a large army of readers crave excitement in its much safer form, in story.

Cloud Atlas (2004) by David Mitchell could be defined as a loosely connected, pyramid-shaped collection of short stories but it is also a novel. The first and last section of *Cloud Atlas* is titled *The Pacific Journal of Adam Ewing*. It is worth sampling the density of Mitchell's invention, to witness how, in this story, his arrangement of incident is designed to prod the adrenal glands of our sample reader.

In the first line, we are whisked away from our humdrum lives, 'I happened on a trail of recent footprints. Through rotting kelp, sea cocoa-nuts & bamboo' (Mitchell, 2004: 3). The ampersand and the word 'journal' in the title tells us we have been jerked back in time. Conjured up for us is a cannibal's banquet, and Dr Goose is collecting the teeth that have been spat out by cannibals after they have swallowed the brains and eyeballs of their victims. The teeth are to be taken to Mayfair, in London, and turned into a set of dentures for the Marchioness of Mayfair, a 'corpse in petticoats' (Mitchell, 2004: 3). It is an act of revenge that Goose intends to wreak on her. He is after her. The chase is on.

The rollercoaster dips sharply as we witness this potential scene: Goose will stand up at the Ambassador's Ball and declare to all and sundry that the Marchioness, the 'scented She-Donkey' (Mitchell, 2004: 4), wears cannibals' teeth, and to prove it he will fling other teeth, more of the same, 'into her tortoise-shell soup tureen & that, sir, that will grant me *my* satisfaction!' (Mitchell, 2004: 4). In one and a quarter pages Mitchell has taken us round the world and back, and given us what amounts to a mini adventure story with the chase after the Marchioness at its heart and that is not even the start of the ride. It is a taster, the training ground for what is to come.

The construct that accelerates us through the story from beginning to end is a race between Dr Henry Goose and Adam Ewing to possess the documents that Ewing travels with — 'Mr Busby's deeds and documents' (Mitchell, 2004: 512), kept in a jackwood trunk, with the key dangling round Ewing's neck.

The race is made suspenseful first by inventing a deadline at which time the race must come to an end. Ewing must come to his senses and realize he is being slowly poisoned by his best friend, the doctor, before the poison kills him, and Dr Goose must commandeer the jackwood trunk containing the documents before the ship reaches San Francisco, when the deeds and the money will be delivered to their rightful owner.

Second, it is made suspenseful with the injection of dramatic irony. We know that Dr Goose is not mending Ewing's ailments, but causing them. 'I melt & itch & blister' (Mitchell, 2004: 515), complains Ewing, thinking he is ill, as the poisons take effect. His blindness to his own slow murder, which happens so clearly in front of our eyes, delivers the delicious excitement of dramatic irony, the same excitement that a child feels while hiding behind a door. 'The whites of my eyes have a lemon-yellow aspect & their rims are reddened and sore. Henry assures me this symptom is welcome, but has obliged my request for an increased dosage of vermicide' (Mitchell, 2004: 493). This race has all the elements that go into the creation of suspense.

There is little excitement to be had in a race that is easily won; whether it is between snails or racehorses or children running to the top of the ridge, the race is only compelling if it is *closely* fought. Mitchell understands this: he has Goose poison Adam Ewing to within an inch of his life and so render him unable to resist the key being taken, but not until the ship is about to dock — the race is neck and neck. In the last few moments available to him, Goose tears open the trunk but it is irrelevant what the results might be. The power of the story, the excitement, has already been delivered. As it happens, Mitchell keeps us on the right side of the moral line and evil is punished: the doctor finds nothing of any value in the trunk. He curses the barely conscious Ewing, 'I have known Irish navvies with more pounds to their name' (Mitchell, 2004: 524). He is barely paid back for the amount he has spent on poisons.

The race is over; therefore the story is over. Mitchell wraps up the tale within a page or two. It is a graceful piece of mimicry, a perfectly realized race structure, arousing excitement.

Even outside this main thrust of the story, the material is arranged in order to excite us. There is a steady, uphill slope on the rollercoaster, for instance, with the wait for the *Prophetess* to be seaworthy. In shorter bursts there are steeper downhills: Ewing's fall into the extinct volcano, to land on a bed of moss, surrounded, as 'hundreds of faces emerged from the perpetual dim, adzed by idolaters into bark, as if Sylvan-spirits were frozen immobile' (Mitchell, 2004: 20). It is followed by an arduous uphill: the climb back out of the volcano. There is a giant swerve sideways: into Bethlehem Bay, in order to swindle 'a cannonball of a man' (Mitchell, 2004: 496), Giles Horrox, out of his store of copra.

Another section of the novel is titled *Half Lives — The First Luisa Rey Mystery*. Adrenaline is once again the chief emotional currency, and a race is at its heart: between various parties who wish to possess the document known as the Sixsmith Report. There are more runners in this race but once again it is the density of invention applied to the *closeness* of the race that demonstrates Mitchell's skill at the form. The race appears to be coming to an end in a bank vault, which houses no less than six hundred safety deposit boxes, and the Sixsmith report is in one of them. Fay Li is in there with her hired goons, but she does not have the number, or the key. She is a close second in the race for this document behind the journalist Luisa Rey, who is arriving now ('*Clipping, female heels*' [Mitchell, 2004: 437]) with the key. Luisa Rey thinks she has won the race. A hand clamped over her mouth, just as she walks in, tells her she has not. Fay Li 'prises the key from the reporter's fingers' (Mitchell, 2004: 437).

Luisa Rey thinks she has lost, but then Fay Li tells her they are on the same side, to all extents and purposes: they both want to see the Sixsmith Report released to the press. Nothing bad will happen to her as long as she does not cause them any trouble. Effectively, Luisa Rey can believe she has won, after all. Yet within a few lines, her new best friend Fay Li turns to the henchmen and speaks in Cantonese. 'Take her to the lock-up. Nothing dirty before you shoot her ... Dispose of the body in the usual way'. Luisa has not won, after all; she has lost, but does not know it. She is taken away. The irony is dreadful.

The race is close; the lead position changes multiple times.

Fay Li 'locates strong box 36/64' (Mitchell, 2004: 438) and opens it, to find the report. The 'flame of jubilation' (Mitchell, 2004: 438) which she feels at her success hints at the coming explosion, because she, also, has failed, just at the point when she believes she's won. She ' ... peers in. A red diode blinks on a neat 4x2 bundle of taped cylinders' (Mitchell, 2004: 438). Bill Smoke has got there before either of them, and he's hitched the report to an explosive device which blows Fay Li — and the report — sky high.

After the fall-out from the explosion, the race can start up again, and Luisa Rey can believe she might win, because it turns out there's a *copy* of the report ...

This excitement is enhanced by the deployment of a moral dimension to the story — an underdog. We care more deeply if our race can be won at the same time as our moral sense is engaged and the gross unfairness of the world overturned. It is almost debilitating to see how effective this is, always. The only time I have seen my wife shout at the television was when Exeter City travelled to Manchester United and came away with a 1–1 draw. She does not care a jot for football. It was a close match; there was an underdog; my wife shouted. It is tiresome, how well the form works.

An uninhibited celebration of the chase-'n-race as a mechanism for arousing excitement is expertly and concisely handled by Mitchell, a literary novelist who enjoys a large readership because of his rare skill at such popular forms of mimesis. One invention after another is vigorously channelled into arousing this one feeling — excitement — and the rich, distinctive writing ensures it stands apart from the clichés which wait to engulf him. However, many good and clever novelists desert the form and will have nothing to do with it because the race or chase has been used to provoke excitement in stories since the dawn of time and in even thinking about it they are faced with a wall of clichés.

Writing exercise no. 13: 'Race back to the house'

Imagine this scenario: a young woman is going to catch a bus when she sees her best friend's boyfriend getting off the bus earlier than expected. She knows that her best friend is currently either lying in bed with another man, or preparing a surprise party, or some such other circumstance that mustn't be discovered.

Orchestrate a race between the friend and the boyfriend with specific attention to the closeness of the race, and the moral issues involved. You will need to investigate the topography, the details of rooms, and doors, and houses and keys, and so on — use these props to help you devise a closer, more exciting race, and use the morality of the situation as a component in the development of the story.

3.2.2. Love

Love's traditional home is in the heart, and if we consult the heart of our volunteer soldier laid out on his slab, and if we look into our own hearts, we can identify when, exactly, we feel the vibration of love most vigorously. As far as sexual love is concerned, it will be at the point when we fall in love, and when we first kiss, when we win the object of our desire, or when we are unable to achieve it, or when we lose it. Intense feelings of love are aroused when the object of our affection is taken away from us, or held at a distance, across which we may not reach.

Outside of the area of sexual love, perhaps it would be at the birth of our child, or at the point, perhaps, when love for a spouse, or for a child, for a sibling, or for a parent, or for a friend, or for the soldier who fights alongside us, achieves for one reason or another a moment of epiphany which lifts the relationship from the humdrum and makes it remarkable in quality.

These observations are commonplace. We are automatic creatures, stuck with identical responses, like Pavlov's dog — more remarkable in our similarities than in our differences. Therefore these forms, or story constructs, are handed to us as the ones which repeatedly work for a broad army of people. It is difficult, in seeking to arouse feelings, to know how to stimulate these repetitive reflexes in such a way as to make the feelings strange and new again, and without arousing resentment in the reader that he or she is being manipulated.

The challenge, therefore, is to the writer's power of narrative invention, before we even begin to tax his or her psychological insight and vocabulary and syntax. Only such passionate engagements with both story and language will enable the author to renew the familiar tropes of story and deliver a fresh and powerful text which engages readers' feelings.

To embrace the cliché — so right, so effective, so many times — the sexual love story searches for devices which keep or wrest the lovers apart: a racial divide, a geographical divide, a class divide, a circumstantial divide, a species divide (in which category my current favourite is the love affair between a bear and a girl in Margo Lanagan's novel, *Tender Morsels* [2008]). The most intense feelings, which of course should be saved until last, occur at the moment of final separation or its polar opposite, union. The problem that faces Mitchell — and all writers — is how to invent such a device when (for western, liberal readers) many of the obstacles formerly encountered by lovers have been torn down. It is not much of an impediment to be married to someone else. Class and poverty should no longer keep people apart, neither should race, nor creed, geography, prejudice against sexual orientation, etc., and not everyone wants to write a ghost story, with death the divide, or to be pushed towards a comedy with — to work the levers — various comical misunderstandings.

Cloud Atlas' second section, titled *Letters From Zedelghem*, is a Moliere-like story of a rogue's scamper through a composer's household set in 1931. Mitchell could have chosen from a range of prejudices and obstacles, but to make the shape of the love-story element in this story suitably light and funny he chose a comical error in understanding to divide his lovers and to explode them apart, in the end. Nonetheless, a feeling of love is aroused in the reader's breast.

Eva, the daughter of the household, a 'snotty duckling' (Mitchell, 2004: 465), has gone away for a while and has returned 'a graceful swan' (Mitchell, 2004: 465). Consequently she and the rogue (known as 'R.F.') begin to enjoy a friendship. A simple phrase dropped from Eva, '(blushing), "I was missing a certain young man I met this June"'

Writing exercise no. 14: 'The hedge'

You are given a very simple mechanism which keeps love apart — a hedge. It can be a garden hedge, or one that borders a field or an estate. The type of love — whether sexual, fraternal, and so on — is up to you, but this short story ends in one of two ways: either the hedge is somehow got through, or cut down, or gone round, or it stays in position and the love — whatever type of love — is denied.

(Mitchell, 2004: 469) means the friendship accelerates into love — R.F *knows* she is describing him. In his own breast he cultivates this passionate love between them, and prepares for their elopement. But his hopes are founded on nothing: she was describing someone else, and in front of our eyes she turns back into the 'snotty duckling'. Mitchell manages to make it funny and heart-breaking at the same time.

To swap from love broken asunder to love brought together, Jane Austen engineers for the whole extent of *Pride and Prejudice* (1813) the widening gap between Darcy and Elizabeth and when she allows Elizabeth to see Darcy's true character her mimicry of this conjoining of love brings love to our own hearts. In Austen's dealings with Elizabeth's family she makes use of the mechanisms by which a moment of understanding, of sorrow or of happiness, lifts loving relationships between the parents, the siblings, the friends, out of the ordinary, and such a lift, an ascension, can only happen if first one has its opposite: lack of understanding, separation, non-communication, conflict of interest. Unhappy strands within the same story are created by sending the direction of travel the other way, from love and understanding to discord and fracture.

This is how feelings of the heart are aroused, whether by Jane Austen or Sebastian Barry or any other writer, in a mimicry of how these feelings are aroused in real life.

3.2.3. Fear

We understand already, with this methodology, that we are facing one cliché after another, and it is worth looking at how one particular writer vigorously embraced the challenge of going through cliché and out the other side.

First, let us locate fear, physically. Its seat — in our volunteer soldier / reader — is in his stomach. It is an emotion sharpened by our flight / fight mechanism: our survival is dependent on its whelming effect. If we consult ourselves, and look into the stomach of our volunteer, we can see we are frightened of the same things: that which is going to hurt us, that which is beyond our control, outside our knowledge and understanding, that which comes at us out of the dark, that which is beyond death — the abyss.

Dickens wished to provoke fear in his short story 'The Haunted House'. The narrator warns us at the outset that he is going to avoid any clichés we might expect.

> Under none of the accredited ghostly circumstances, and environed by none of the conventional ghostly surroundings, did I first make acquaintance with the house which is the subject of this Christmas piece. I saw it in daylight, with the sun upon it. There was no wind, nor rain, no lightning, no thunder, no awful or unwonted circumstance, of any kind, to heighten its effect. (Byatt, 1998: 18)

Having thrown out the pathetic fallacy, Dickens then invites in plenty of his own clichés. The narrator finds out from a young man called Ikey that there is an "'Ooded woman with an howl." "Do you mean a cry?" "No, an owl." "A hooded woman with an owl. Dear me'" (Byatt, 1998: 22).

Other clichés flood in, to comical effect: the hooded woman was murdered while the owl hooted, there is a bell that rings by itself.

But now Dickens begins to invent things that are not clichés. A former occupant 'Master B' had the habit of pulling off the wallpaper in his room. The narrator, John, moves into the house with his sensible sister and a clutch of servants with comical names — The Odd Girl, Streaker and a deaf stable-man, Bottles. These are not clichés: the Odd Girl 'sees eyes' (Byatt, 1998: 26), while Streaker silently goes about her duties with eyes filled with tears, and Cook repeats over and over whom she wants her silver pocket watch to go to when she dies.

These are unusual, distinctive inventions, yet still Dickens will shortly toss them aside.

The narrator, John, and his sister are the practical ones. If Master B's bell rings all by itself, then it must be due to mice chewing through the cable or whatever, and he will pull it from its fittings. If the wallpaper un-peels itself, then he will glue it back up. However, the servants are a different matter. They are petrified. But John is dismissive of their fears,

> ... the contagion of suspicion and fear was among us, and there is no such contagion under the sky. Hooded woman? According to the accounts, we were in a perfect Convent of hooded women. Noises? With that contagion downstairs, I myself have sat in this dismal parlour, listening, until I have heard so many and such strange noises, that they would have chilled my blood if I had not warmed it by dashing out to make discoveries... It was in vain to do anything. It was in vain to be frightened, for the moment in one's own person, by a real owl ...

Of course we sense for ourselves the inversion that is about to happen: it is the servants who are sensible, who see what is going on.

John and his sister get rid of the servants and hire new ones, and the same happens, so they get rid of those.

The only servant immune to all the noises, the hauntings, is the deaf stable man, Bottles, who keeps on steadily eating potatoes and pie.

The volume of frightening effects — both clichés and non-clichés — are attached to the volume of servants, who are now dispatched. This is Dickens' vigorous attack on clichés, on all imaginary effects. John's sister suggests, 'Have no servants.'

Instead, John and his sister now invite a select group of sensible people of their own class to live here and report what is going on truthfully. To decide on which bedrooms they should occupy, they draw lots. All is well; they have some excellent food, and exercise. There is a howling noise made by the wind in the weathercock but they go up on the roof in the wind and the rain and quite enjoy themselves taking the weathercock down. And then the chimney cowl. 'Another night, they cut a sobbing and gulping water pipe away' (Byatt, 1998: 33).

The clichés having gone, now it is time for Dickens' invention. John's lot was to sleep in Master B's room, and he is pursued in his dreams by everything to do with 'B'. The hauntings, instead of being exterior — owls, and noises, and bells ringing — have become interior. John shaves one morning and sees 'B' in the mirror instead of his own reflection. The delirium descends. At night, he must sleep in the same bed as B's skeleton. It is terrifying. John is 'lying down and rising up with the skeleton allotted to me for my mortal companion' (Byatt, 1998: 43).

Dickens invites in cliché in order to battle with it, dispense with it, and go beyond it. We will only ever be scared of the same things as we ever were; the writer's task is to re-cycle with masterful invention.

Dickens connects one solitary wire to his readers' stomach, and, having at first set himself the task of deliberately flinging from him all clichés, pours down that wire a current of fear.

We have finished with our volunteer reader-soldier's body — that is to say, below the neck. These foregoing forms of emotion are the animalistic ones, evident in beasts as well as in man, and they correspond to the more populist, sensual genres. I do not mean to say they are easier to write; in fact their relative simplicity compared to the more cerebral emotions means the clichés are crowded into a narrower sluice or crossing point. A writer enters the arena and is immediately trampled underfoot by other writers. Only invention, technical skill, and authoritative phrase-making will repel the reader's resentment.

Now we move upwards to the head, specifically the brain, a prize area, the seat of this consciousness that we, as a species, have developed to such a pitch of self-awareness that it takes us far from the animal kingdom. All feeling, emotion, thought, all reading and viewing of story, might be considered to be registered here, but it is the seat, the home, of three particular feelings: the first is curiosity; the next two are the twin pillars of feeling, the king and queen of emotion, who wear the twin masks that have long been the iconic signifiers of dramatic writing, one with the downturned mouth, the other with the laughing smile — comedy and tragedy. The feelings they intend to arouse are laughter and pity.

3.2.4. Curiosity

We might discuss whether or not curiosity is an emotion, but I would ask that it be accepted: curiosity is an emotion. In the previous analogy, The Alchemist, I described how curiosity is the feeling attached to our species-specific compulsion to perceive and develop logic. Our delight in satisfying our curiosity leads to the success of mystery stories as well as the various histories (including biography) — in other words, what happened to whom, and why. How the world works.

A mystery story sets out first to arouse and then answer our curiosity. Curiosity is easy enough to invoke: a question is planted that invites us, more or less compellingly, to answer it. In *Watchmen* (Gibbons and Moore, 1986), for example, it is first of all the strange little yellow disc that we see in all the opening frames, from one perspective or another, large in the frame or small, until it slips down the drain.

More challenging, after invoking mystery, is to make the filling-in of the puzzle interesting, compelling in its display of logic, resonant with meaning and, in the end, complete.

I have left David Mitchell's *Cloud Atlas* behind, but I want to bring it back in front of us now very briefly because it makes for an interesting example as far as curiosity is concerned: this pleasurable emotion is provided not only inside the pages of the stories but also in the way in which they are fitted together: the journal written by Adam Ewing becomes the torn-in-half manuscript that prevents the bed from wobbling in *Letters From...* Our curiosity is aroused when we meet the paragraph, 'I came across a curious volume ... From what little I can glean, it's the edited journal of a voyage from Sydney to San Francisco named Adam Ewing' (Mitchell, 2004: 64).

At this point a question is posed in our minds: how will this connection be forged, what deft touch is going to weld this story to the next one, and where and in what shape will this fictional relay-race of documents, of writing, end up? The letters themselves become embedded in *The First Luisa Rey Mystery*, the story of which, in its turn, becomes a typescript clutched by the unscrupulous literary agent Timothy Cavendish in *The Ghastly Ordeal*... and so on.

The story knows more than us. Having advertised the gap in the puzzle, it provides the piece that will fit. The whole construct changes shape even as we are invited to stitch it together, and finally, with the last piece, the picture is complete, and it shows all its lines and colours; curiosity is satisfied, the display of logic is enchanting.

In itself it is not a difficult thing for Mitchell to have pulled off, but for the duration of the work this engagement of curiosity has been a gentle background hum — the sound of the kinetic force that binds the disparate stories into a whole.

3.2.5. Pity

Pity and laughter are the most difficult feelings to evoke. Pity — the feeling that tragedy must look for — is aroused by the readers' perception of suffering when a writer puts in front of them all that is wrong with the world. But when reading a novel, a fictional story, we are in recreational mode: we read for pleasure. How is it possible for a reader to look on human suffering, and yet take pleasure? The answer is: if the moral angle is attended to, and we are safe within the confines of a novel, feelings of pity can be enjoyed.

Again we look to real life for the shape that pity takes. What is most wrong with the world — what is most pitiful? That a man has to die, surely. Burckhardt has it that, 'A tragedy — to define it very simply — is a *killing poem*; it is designed toward the end of bringing a man to some sort of destruction' (Burckhardt, 1968: 15).

But more pitiful than a man dying is a woman dying, and more grave still is if a child dies. It is most sad when a female child dies, and it is sadder beyond pity if it is not her fault, if her death (suffering) is unmerited, and if such an injustice combines with inevitability it adds weight to our moral outrage and arouses further sadness. If it is not her own fault because of who she is, because of a flaw in her character that is no more than the extension of a virtue, then the iron hand of character (in which we are all trapped through no fault of our own) prescribes her fate, and all previous sadness is doubled because we add our own sadness into the mix.

This is the shape of tragedy, of pity; it is how it works in all of us and we can, if we wish, borrow it and lift it across into our fiction.

It is not in *Cloud Atlas* but in the first 90 pages of *number9dream*, also by David Mitchell, that we find a perfectly realized tragedy. It is the story of the competition between the child twins, Anju and Eijie.

Mitchell introduces the female twin, Anju, with the line 'Anju climbed trees like a cat' (Mitchell, 2001: 44). The story is told by her brother, and his use of the past tense warns us that his sister Anju is dead, and his cutting off the head of the thunder god 'for what he did to "Anju"' (Mitchell, 2001: 43) tells us the end of the story at the start. The thunder god killed Anju. All that is left is to find out how, and to feel the pity of it.

The twins, brother and sister, compete with each other on various fronts. On page 58, they argue over a theory which proposes that, if you dream that you're falling, and in your dream you hit the ground, you will in fact die. '"Rubbish!" "Scientists proved it!"' Anju wins the argument and ' ... enjoys her victory in silence' (Mitchell, 2001: 58). The competitions between them, physical and mental, are a continual undercurrent — 'but I know Anju wants me to ask "Where?" so I don't' (Mitchell, 2001: 45) and, 'I was born first so you have to do what I say' (Mitchell, 2001: 46) and 'we stare at each other and the first one to look away wins' (Mitchell, 2001: 51) and 'Anju snaps at me. "You're not the only one who can do grown-up things!"' (Mitchell, 2001: 64). It is normally Anju who is victorious – 'She wins — she always does ... ' (Mitchell, 2001: 51), often because Eijie lets her, or because he is less physically brave: '"Don't," is all I can blurt' (Mitchell, 2001: 46), he says, when Anju dangles upside down from a tree. This is her great virtue — she is competitive, bold; and she is a winner.

There is one thing, though, at which she cannot beat her brother — football. He is ambitious. 'I will play for Japan on my twentieth birthday against Brazil in the World Cup Final' (Mitchell, 2001: 53) and she cannot compete when he announces that he is going across the water on the ferry to play in an important match. 'You're jealous because I'm going to Kagoshima and you're not' (Mitchell, 2001: 53). The stage is set, in terms of character, for Anju's competitive streak — a good thing, which we've admired so much — to stretch one inch too far, and to turn, in front of our eyes, from a virtue to a flaw in her character, for her to become not just competitive, but over-competitive. This evokes pity because the vice (something wrong with her) grows out of a virtue (what's good about her), which means she cannot be blamed. She is a victim of her own character. The irony of it ensures our reaction is cathartic, and it increases our love for Anju precisely because we are the same, we have the vices of our virtues. This is the tradition of the tragic character, and it is a tradition that has developed because readers and audiences, over thousands of years, have gained pleasure from it.

Mitchell has concentrated on the building of the unfairness of the twins' misfortune, just as much as he concentrated on the closeness of the races previously described in *Cloud Atlas*. Once again it is unfairness that is the wind in the sails of the vessel that carries us through the story.

The background circumstances, even, in which Eijie and Anju find themselves, make them undeserving of further misfortune: Mitchell is careful not to make them orphans because that is too obvious a play for our sympathy, but in some ways they are worse than orphans, with a drunk mother and an absent father. It therefore becomes even more important that they have each other. They are twins, which fact adds to this reaction. They feed each other — 'Want a champagne bomb?' asks Eijie. ' ... you need a midnight snack to build you up' (Mitchell, 2001: 57). Any parent, or keeper of pets, knows that an important sponsor of love is feeding. And it is not just food that they give each other — 'my new baseball cap which Anju bought me with her pocket money from Uncle Tarmac' (Mitchell, 2001: 66). And they are kind to each other. 'I wipe Anju's tears. They are so warm' (Mitchell, 2001: 47). They must not, should not be separated.

It is not only in the background circumstances that their misfortune is cast: Eijie only prays to the thunder god because he wants to play well in a football match. When he offers the thunder god anything the latter might want in return, he does not think, in a million years, that it will be his sister that the thunder god takes. He is the architect of his own loss, but he did not deserve to be. He wishes to climb to the thunder god to ask for help in getting to the World Cup because the football initiative is attached, in our minds and theirs, to finding their father. 'Finding our father is big fry. No fry is bigger for Anju and me' (Mitchell, 2001: 79). Anju's unseen attempt to swim as far as the whalestone is brave. It is to answer — to match — her brother's success in being picked for the team. Her competitive streak — previously so wonderful a thing — does not deserve to be punished for stretching this one inch further.

And every step of the way, there are warnings that we, the readers, can see, but they cannot – 'Ghosts can fly' and 'Ghosts are dead' (Mitchell, 2001: 47). ' ... parts of Anju are so dark she isn't even here' (Mitchell, 2001: 47). '"Don't go to Kagoshima tomorrow, Eijie." "I have to go. I'm in defence." "*Don't go*"' (Mitchell, 2001: 64). The pearly snake has been seen, and their grandma says it only ever appears to warn of an impending death. We hear yet more warnings in Eijie's explanations as to why some people climb the steps to the thunder god, to ask for ' ... solace for dead relatives' (Mitchell, 2001: 67). Further warnings echo through the text: 'dead children live on these steps' (Mitchell, 2001: 69). At the top of the steps, just about to meet the thunder god, Eijie gongs the bell three times. 'The third gong is to slam shut for ever the iron doors' (Mitchell, 2001: 70). When he approaches the shrine, the thunder god's face ' ... is hatred, typhoon and nightmare all knotted up. I can't back out now. He's awake' (Mitchell, 2001: 70).

We already know it is Anju who will die, but more importantly, it is the extent to which she does not deserve to, that counts for the evocation of pity, and the stream of warnings adds to the impression that her drowning is both inevitable and undeserved. It should not happen.

Eijie and Anju, being twins, are two halves of the same person, and his tragic flaw, the vice of his virtue, is the same as hers: his competitive spirit. In order to improve his chances of winning the football match he makes his fatal deal with the thunder god — '"When I'm a famous soccer player I'll, uh, come back and rebuild your shrine and

> Writing exercise no. 15: 'The Pitiful Mrs Lambert'
>
> The purpose of this exercise is to evoke the feeling of pity in your reader.
>
> You are given a character, Mrs Lambert, who is a kind person.
>
> Invent a series of incidents in which Mrs Lambert displays the virtue of kindness to another person of your own devising.
>
> Make Mrs Lambert even more kind — until she is kind to a fault.
>
> Invent a series of further incidents between these same two characters, until Mrs Lambert's kindness becomes such a weakness, that it leads to her downfall.

stuff. Until then, anything that I can give you, you can have. Take it. You don't have to ask me, just take it." The silence sighs. "Anything?" "Anything"' (Mitchell, 2001: 70).

Mitchell provides a long, quiet moment, in the middle of the frenetic tree-climbing and so on, in which the import of this deal is felt. 'The silence lasts nine days and nine nights' (Mitchell, 2001: 70). And then the thunder-god gives his answer. 'Done' (Mitchell, 2001: 70). A final warning chases us into what we already know will happen, ' ... the ghosts of the dead children are dissolving in the first sunlight' (Mitchell, 2001: 71). Eijie will score a goal, and Anju will try and swim to the whalestone, and drown. Compared to our certainty as to what is going to happen, Eijie's lack of fore-knowledge arouses pathos. 'My sister'll be walking down to meet me.' (Mitchell, 2001: 88). Mitchell toys with our expectations. 'Anju's foot thump ... No, it was only the old house.' (Mitchell, 2001: 68) but in the end he must deliver. 'Then, with sickening certainty, I think of the whalestone. To get even with me.' (Mitchell, 2001: 90). He runs to see if her swimming costume is there — but it is gone. He remembers his promise to the thunder god, and the tragedy strikes him, fells him, as well as us. 'I get the words out before everything crashes down. "Look in the sea."' (Mitchell, 2001: 90). In revenge Eijie not only cuts off the thunder god's head, he picks it up and lugs it all the way to the cliff's edge and, within sight of the whalestone, he hurls it over the cliff, to condemn it to the same fate as that suffered by his sister.

To witness suffering that is deserved repels us, in fiction, unless it is brief and conducted in a spirit of revenge. In contrast to this, undeserved suffering strikes against our moral centre, and and the degree to which the suffering is unfair, and the degree to which it is inevitable, directly controls (like a valve) the outpouring of cathartic pity in our reader.

It is a sensation we can enjoy because it is safely contained within the pages of a story. In real life, like fear and excitement, we instinctively understand that pity might be complicated, and it might cost us. In a story, with the paper-thin membrane between reality and fiction protecting us, pity can be pleasurable, a free exercise of feeling what is wrong with the world.

3.2.6. Laughter

Comedy, like tragedy, defines for us what is wrong with the world, but in comedy we laugh at what is wrong instead of mourn it. Comedy and tragedy are two strands of the same rope, a tightrope which is stretched across — an inch above — the mire that is all human suffering, except the comic writer takes us across the tightrope facing the opposite direction from the tragedian, and provokes laughter instead of pity.

This morning I woke up and immediately picked up the book I had fallen asleep over, David Nicholls' *One Day* (2009). The Trotskyite Gary Nutkin takes Emma out on a first date, a Peter Greenaway double bill. Gary Nutkin waits 'until four hours in before reaching across and absent-mindedly placing his hand on her left breast as if adjusting a dimmer switch' (Nicholls, 2009: 22). It is the *four hours* and then the *adjusting*, as well as the callous lack of sensuality in '*dimmer switch*', that makes it such a perfectly wrong move. There is a lot wrong with Gary Nutkin.

As in tragedy, the moral question, the question of fairness, is of central importance in the successful generation of humour. In *Cloud Atlas*, in the comic section given the Wodehousian title, *The Ghastly Ordeal of Timothy Cavendish*, Mitchell puts dear old Tim with his trousers down, sitting on the toilet, when the two thugs Jarvis and

Eddie break in to ask for the money he owes them. He has to greet them while still sitting on the toilet.

> 'Gentlemen, I'm happy to pay a negotiated consideration, but the law ... '
> Jarvis whistled through his teeth. 'Will the law help a man of your years bounce back from multiple spinal fractures, Timothy?'
> Eddie: 'Men of your age don't bounce. They splat.'
> I fought with all my might, but my sphincter was no longer my own and a cannonade fired off. Amusement or condescension I could have borne, but my tormentors' pity signified my abject defeat. The toilet chain was pulled. (Mitchell, 2004: 157)

We laugh, but if we are to be free to enjoy our laughter it is important to us that Tim deserves his punishment (scamming money from a gangster), and that although Jarvis and Eddie threaten grave injury, they inflict no more pain than pinching Tim's cheek while he sits on the bog. The embarrassment (what is wrong) can invoke our laughter because the morality has been finely judged. If the pain, if the wrongness, is too grave, laughter will be replaced by dismay.

The cleverest comedians press hardest against this boundary, because it is where the richest, most dangerous laughs can be found. It is an individual response, unique in each of us, that depends on our experience of right and wrong, which is attached to our experience of suffering.

For instance, the comedian Frankie Boyle can say that a female TV presenter's face looks like it is reflected in the back of a spoon and most of us are free to laugh, but for the girl and her mother, even if they see the same truth, the wrongness is too sharp, painful; suddenly they are facing the other way, they will not laugh.

Comedy and tragedy are the King and Queen of dramatic writing due to their special relationship with right and wrong. They stand on each side of the steps which lead up to the giant blank page, or canvas, on which all stories are written, and fairness — our sense of right and wrong — is what the canvas is made of.

3.3. Spiritual needs

This third category of morale, the spiritual category, is concerned with belief — with what an army commander can persuade his soldiers to believe, in order to control what they think of as right and wrong.

We can step back into the world of our analogy: the murderous world of the Burma campaigns, where each one of us would have killed other men and women, often, and in as great a number as we possibly could.

The misdeeds of the Japanese, from Pearl Harbour onwards, created the righteousness in the hearts of the allies which allowed them to drop atomic bombs on Nagasaki and Hiroshima. Morality is a moveable feast. The man or woman who would consider it wrong to kill one person can be persuaded it is right to kill hundreds of thousands if the circumstances are arranged in a particular way.

The novelist, also, must pay close attention to the sense of right and wrong that is inherent in their army of readers. And the skilful writer will take delight in doing so.

Morality, like logic, is uniquely important to mankind as a species. In the previous analogy I attached a description of the importance of logic to the image of the owls hunting at night; similarly I might attach the importance of morality in humans to the ant species. Whereas ants have a collective intelligence, a collective set of behaviours, that depend on scent or on the tappings of their antennae to allow them to determine their task, and their grouping, and how to reach food and return home, we have collectives of morality, based on different schemes of right and wrong. In ants, the use of pheromones is supernaturally well developed: they have a food pheromone, which identifies a route towards food that diminishes when that food source is depleted; they have a different pheromone for the route back from food. They have an alarm pheromone, released by a crushed ant, which summons its neighbours and angers them so they will attack; they have a propoganda pheromone, which confuses enemy ants and encourages them to fight among themselves; they have a mating pheromone.

Likewise our sense of morality is highly tuned; both within our group and between groups we instantly combine impressions of language, clothing, physical appearance and behaviour into something as quick, in effect, as a pheromone, and we deconstruct it (in what way is this person 'right', 'in what way is he or she 'wrong') to determine if this other person is a member of the group — or the sub-group within the group — in which we currently choose to situate ourselves. It is a constantly engaged function, special to the human brain. Just as we constantly measure and investigate cause-and-effect, we are compelled always to adjust and measure the relationship between right and wrong, both in ourselves and in those around us.

The mimicry of this continually engaged function is an important part of the writer's work. Truman Capote's *Breakfast At Tiffany's* (1958) demonstrates how an author might do so, to good effect.

We first encounter Holly Golightly when she returns to her apartment block late at night and, because she has once again forgotten her downstairs key, she presses Mr Yunioshi's bell and wakes him up — as usual. Our moral judgement is invoked, to a small extent: she is a little thoughtless, always to wake Mr Yunioshi.

Holly placates Mr Yunisohi by offering something in return, '... if you promise not to be angry ... I might let you take those pictures we mentioned' (Capote, 1958/1961: 16).

The moral sense changes: whereas Holly was formerly in the wrong, in a mild way, for carelessly waking up a neighbour, now Mr Yunioshi is more seriously in the wrong for having tried to engineer the taking of insalubrious photographs of Holly. Holly herself is perhaps even more entrenched in wrong-doing, for entertaining the prospect of such photographs, and for using the temptation of them to soothe Mr Yunioshi. It is the author's tease with us, as much as it is Holly's teasing of Mr Yunioshi. 'When?' he asks, and she slurs her reply, 'Sometime' (Capote, 1958/1961: 17).

The important, final result (for us) is that she will not ever succumb to Mr Yunioshi's camera. Our initial moral judgement, that she is in the wrong, will be overturned. Furthermore, the 'short and vast' (Capote, 1958/1961: 16) man who accompanies her to the door of her apartment, and who assumes he has bought his way into some class of sexual relations with Holly, is left with the door shut in his face. She denies him. Yet, as he is going down the stairs, thumping the wall in frustration, she calls down to him that, in paying for drinks and food for her and five of her friends this evening, he has not paid enough. "'The next time a girl wants a little powder-room change,'" she scolds him, "take my advice, darling: *don't* give her twenty cents!'" (Capote, 1958/1961: 18).

These are the first few steps in a footloose dance with morality that characterizes Capote's portrayal of Holly Golightly. He tempts us to think ill of her, only to deliver instead her saintliness. In this way, he forces us — we are like the ants, tap-tapping — repeatedly to correct our judgement of Holly; always, in the end, it is towards the 'good', and thus he sponsors our heartfelt love for her.

On page 30 she climbs into the narrator's bed, not to make love with him, but for warmth. While she thinks that he is asleep, she strokes his cheek and calls him the name of another, unknown man, Fred, 'Where are you, Fred? Because it's cold. There's snow in the wind' (Capote, 1958/1961: 30).

The narrator is given this special name, and we are invited to think it is the name of an ex-lover — yet another man. But it turns out to be the name of her brother, and her love for him is altruistic, pure. The dance back and forth continues. Capote teases our moral judgement of this character. Just as the skilful author performs, in his writing, an enchanting display of logic, so does Capote make an enchanting display of morality.

We learn from Holly's agent that she was picked up and groomed for almost certain Hollywood stardom, but she turned around at the last moment and cancelled the big screen test because, as she explains, ' ... you got to want it to be good and I don't want it' (Capote, 1958/1961: 34). This is the girl who, we have learned, likes nothing better than to be the centre of attention, yet she has turned down what we would have snapped up for ourselves. Our previous moral judgement, that she is an attention-seeking actress-type, is overturned. She is a better person than we are.

On pages 36-8 we learn of her scattergun kindness when she invites old people, strangers, to her party, each of whom thinks they are the only invitee, while at the same time we learn that she is using the party to show off her hooking-up with the notorious gossip-column heir, Rusty Trawler. Back on the 'good' side of the moral line, she is paying noble attention to the narrator's career in making sure he collars the attention of the same Hollywood agent that she has already disappointed. The density of the inventive cloth is what is remarkable here. Every inch of it is designed to clothe and then unclothe our moral perception of Holly Golightly.

It is the appearance of another 'suspicious specimen' (Capote, 1958/1961: 61), among the many other men who hang on to Holly's skirts, that provides the next big escalation in the sweep of our back-and-forth moral judgement of her. This man, who is spotted waiting for her outside the apartment block, is '… in his early fifties with a hard, weathered face, grey, forlorn eyes. He wore an old sweat-stained grey hat … '. It turns out he is not her father, as our narrator thinks, but her husband, five years on the road trying to track her down. And now we suspect a tawdry tale. Holly Golightly will turn out to be a child-bride from the deep south, married to a paedophile.

In fact, what emerges is a love story as tender as you could like. This man, her legitimate husband, whom she loves, in a way, is the only man that she sleeps with, before she sends him on his way.

These back-and-forths across the moral line are perhaps only the training ground for the biggest one of all, which happens on pages 70–4. Holly has been consorting with Rusty Trawler, the rich, much-married playboy *often accused of pro-Nazi sympathies*, and we are expecting to hear of their engagement. Instead, we hear from a gossip column about his engagement to Mag, a beautiful cover girl from Arkansas.

Holly has a fit. It was 'as though tigers were loose in Holly's apartment. A riot of crashing glass, of rippings and fallings and overturned furniture' (Capote, 1958/1961: 71).

Capote leads us to think that she is grieving over Rusty Trawler. This puts her in the wrong, in our eyes and in the narrator's eyes. He asks, 'Why should she have a fit over Rusty?' (Capote, 1958/1961: 73)

The switch is revealed via a scrumpled-up piece of paper on the floor. It is a telegram that she had a fit over. The telegram was sent by Doc Golightly, her old husband whom she has sent back to Texas.

Writing exercise no. 16: 'The smart car'

Take one of your characters for a drive. Put him (or her) behind the steering wheel of an old banger, and while he drives, you can interrogate his thoughts, his situation, and the events that have recently happened in your story or that might be about to happen.

Now write the sequence again, and put him (or her) behind the wheel of a very new, luxury car, of some description.

After leaving the material to sit for a while, read both again and measure your own reaction, as a reader, to the evidence of wealth.

The telegram reads, *'Fred killed in action overseas stop your husband and children join in* the sorrow of our mutual loss stop letter follows love doc' (Capote, 1958/1961: 74).

She does not care a fig for Rusty Trawler. She is grieving over the death of her *brother*, whose name she has given to our narrator (and therefore to us). The moral pendulum swings the other way in its most extensive arc yet — and stays there. In our eyes she has become angelic. We put her at the top of the Christmas tree — that is the feeling aroused in us by Capote's clever manipulation of our moral sense.

In 1943, in Burma, Field Marshal Slim was able to use the horrors perpetrated on allied troops by the Japanese in order to bolster the moral righteousness of his troops. For instance, a Japanese advance-guard had overrun a field hospital, killed all the doctors and nurses and transported the wounded back behind their own lines, where they were tortured for information. In another incident, the Japanese dressed as Burmese villagers and lay in wait for an allied scouting party and took them captive. The following morning they strung up the allied soldiers and used them for bayonet practice, in order to intimidate the local Burmese. These immoral acts — immoral even in the world of war — fuelled the righteousness of the allied forces as they prepared to re-take Burma.

The allies had rested, and retrained. They had learned how to fight in the jungle. They had learned the use of the hook, and with the use of Wingate's gliders they now employed it on a grander, bolder scale. Morale was solid. Feelings ran high. In this way they turned defeat into victory.

This analogy, The Invasion, proposes that a writer should be compared to an army commander, but the difference with writing, of course, is that we have all the time we need to prepare, to put in place the strategies that will cover the ground, and defeat the enemy.

But — who is the writer's enemy? There is the ground we have to cover, to lead our army of readers across, and we have to create our victory, but whom are we fighting against?

The only possible answer is other writers, who might cover the ground before we get there.

4. THE DONKEY'S HEAD

The previous analogies have described the practice of writing fiction as an act of interpretive mimesis; the two hereafter concern themselves with the practice of *re*-writing. For some writers (myself included) this constitutes the bulk of the work in terms of time taken.

There are only two things that can be 'wrong' with a novel, or any given passage or thread in a novel: either something is included that ought to have been left out, or something is missing that should have been included. This applies to the large scale re-write — whole characters or plot strands — as well as the microscopic, line-by-line edit: should that comma be removed?

The forthcoming analogy, The Donkey's Head, concerns itself with what should be cut from a text to make it more effective. Its remit is more closely defined: I want to look at those extraneous pieces of writing that stay there because the author loves them too much. They are the most ruinous.

In Shakespeare's *A Midsummer Night's Dream* (circa 1590) Puck is briefed by Oberon to place a drop of ointment in Titania's eye, and this drop carries a spell: Titania will fall in love with the first creature she sets eyes on when she awakes, 'Be it ounce, or cat, or bear, /Pard, or boar with bristled hair' (II.iii.29). Thereby she enters into a state of enchantment: in love, but unable to see that the man she loves has the head of a donkey.

A state of enchantment will — should — steal over us when we sit down to *read* fiction. Jack Ouseby imagines:

> A child is reading. She has tied a torch to the bed-head so that the light focuses on her book and does not disturb her younger sister, asleep in the bed next to hers. She is so absorbed in the reading she seems to have created a force field around herself, a palpable energy which holds her tightly inside the world the story-maker has created. (Ouseby, 1992: 40)

The poet Oliver Reynolds also describes the enchantment of reading:

> ... the strangest recession:
> I am there but not there.
> I am reading.
>
> My body dwindles.
> Thinned by text it becomes Euclidean:
> It has position but no magnitude:
>
> An hour later, it returns;
> Slowly, as if dropping by parachute (Reynolds, 2010)

The same spell envelops the 'story-maker,' the writer, when he or she sits down to compose fiction. The writer, in picking up her pen, conjures up a private, enchanted space. It feels like waking up, like coming alive to the beauty of the world. Titania-as-writer stirs from her sleep, and both her eye and her ear become finely tuned, and she is enchanted with what is in front of her, underneath her pen.

A text — a novel — will cast this spell over both its writer and its reader if the adapted mimicry of real life contained within its pages is sufficiently artful.

However, a danger lurks — that the spirit of enchantment is successfully cast over the writer alone. Titania-as-writer gazes on her work and sees something that can only be loved; 'Mine ear is much enamoured of thy note /So is mine eye enthralled by thy shape' (III.i.140–3). But everyone else sees a donkey.

And I use Titania, rather than Narcissus, for this analogy because it is the blindness that interests me. Narcissus was not blind; he was simply unable to stop admiring his own reflection, and that was his downfall. This is not the case here; we are not particularly vain, at least not beyond a commonplace vanity. A trick has been played on us. A drop has been put in our eye that makes us blind. We will see the work clearly when the antidote is applied.

I want to linger for a while on the subject of enchantment. In *Shakespeare and the Popular Tradition in the Theater* (1967/1978), Robert Weimann describes how ritual enchantment was created in primitive peoples by the mimicry of the most important areas of their experience, usually related to survival.

> The water dwellers of Tierra del Fuego, for example, have their canoe play, the Bambuti pygmies their jungle-hunting game, the Tasmanians a seal game, and the Kemirai of New South Wales a kangaroo game. At this level of culture *mimesis* arises out of a community in which there is little division of labour; the 'spectators' take part in the game or join in the acting. The unity of player and audience is complete when each participant shares in the indivisible process of primitive living. (Weimann, 1967/1978: 2)

This solidarity — when audience and performers are as one — begins to divide when he spins us forwards to a more developed culture, which has devised theatre — those who enjoy ritual mimesis now separate into two groups — those who perform the mimicry (the actors) and those who watch it (the audience), and 'The imitating subject, or ego, imposes his own standards onto the object and the resultant representation is, as Aristotle was to note later, not merely a passive reproduction of something given, that is, not a simple imitation. It is no accident that the verb corresponding to the Greek word for "actor" — *hypokrites* — means "to interpret," and less often "to answer"' (Weimann, 1967/1978: 2).

Nonetheless, audience and actors still occupy the same space.

With the printed word, and the novel, the separation between the person 'performing' the mimesis (the story-teller) and audience (reader) separates further: they are no longer in the same room. They might be apart by thousands of miles and hundreds of years. Thereby, it has become an intensely private ritual. It is still mimesis — the novel is a manipulation of how life works — but now it is a communion between the inside of one person's head (the writer's) directly, via the silent music of words, to the inside of another person's head (the reader's). Both parties, all being well, should enter into the same state of enchantment, but they arrive separately, from different directions, and from a long way off. The territory where they meet Philip Pullman calls 'The Borderlands' (Pullman, 2009).

Jane Smiley describes what it is like when a reader arrives at The Borderlands and finds everything is to her satisfaction:

> ... the joy of meeting up with the author's mind is so intense that it hardly seems possible that it must be private, that it can't be communicated, or even expressed. When a novel has two hundred thousand words, then it is possible for the reader to experience two hundred thousand delights, and to turn back to the first page of the book and experience them all over again, perhaps more intensely. (Smiley, 2006: 279)

However, it does not always turn out so well. It is the loss of direct physical contact between the subject and the object of the mimesis, together with the intensely private, egotistical nature of the act of writing, that partly accounts for the particular type of blindness that I am going to describe in this analogy: when the writer, alone in his cave, is enchanted, but the reader is not. The only proof against this eventuality is to become the fresh, unknowing visitor to our work, as if we ourselves approached The Borderland from the opposite direction, that of the innocent reader. This act of becoming 'other' must be the ambition of the re-writing writer. When it works, it is like a curtain being drawn back to reveal to you something you have always known, but until that moment have been unable to see.

It is not strange to report that many of the revelations concerning the re-writing of *What The Children Saw* came to me while I was in another form of enchantment, or trance. No doubt we all have particular circumstances when the mind, like in Reynolds' poem, becomes 'there but not there'. For me, those occasions happen when my physical self is engaged in automatic, repetitive procedures — when I run, and when I swim, or when I drive.

1. Run (2 hours 11 minutes)

The running shoes are light and foamy underfoot. My footfall is sprung, optimistic. The coat also is weightless, a plastic skein of bright red. If I fall and break or sprain an ankle, I will be a drop of blood against the dun of the landscape and it will catch the helicopter's eye.

I am not yet thinking of the work; instead I swap three maps in my head in order to choose a route: long, middle or short. It is cool enough — the clouds turn the summer's colour into a metallic monochrome and the air arrives lazily from the frozen north. I decide on the long run. I will start now, with this stride, and I will reach the end without stopping.

It is a one-track lane, the tarmac silvery in the morning damp. It winds between the dew-laden hedgerows. One foot kicks in front of the other; both go about their back and forth. The hands are kept low, around the height of the hips, and they echo the feet's movement. They service the upright, keep the pendulum balanced, and they have a flywheel effect, giving momentum.

I am still not thinking of the work; I am occupied with measuring the systems, like pressing the 'check' button in the car. That crease of pain in the calf is a left-over from an injury and will ease. The knees do not thud too hard. The right shoelace is knotted too tight but I cannot be bothered to stop. The heaviness of last night's drink will be blown away if I keep going.

The gate is a series of noises: the chink of the opened latch, a squeaking hinge, the thud of wood against post, a rattle as the latch is replaced. A further, gentle incline must be faced, but there will be no more tarmac for the next two hours and instead underfoot is raw track: beaten earth and small stones, and the sponge of the soaked moor, packed with the roots of grasses — cow clover, eaver and cocksfoot — while on each side gorse bushes gather ominously — each time you look away, they appear to grow one more of themselves, and come closer. Their yellow flowers offer a gardenia-like scent.

Still I have not reached the zone where I will think of the work. Instead I will shrug on the mantle of the landscape, like getting dressed in familiar clothes.

Behind — across my shoulders — lies the Devon plain, a patchwork of green, worked over more closely than a garden, that stretches for 40 miles until it reaches Exmoor, and there is one dark spot I turn briefly to look for: the Teign gorge, its steep sides all rust and brown, commandeered by Castle Drogo.

In front, like a wave that one rides up in a small boat, is the near horizon, just a few hundred yards away, which then drops underfoot to offer a giddy view: strings of tors along a horizon now miles distant, a basin of land gathering five streams, the Fernworthy plantation like an unlikely haircut on one side. There is no mankind, only fauna and flora, one might think, for miles, but this apparent absence of the human hand is deceptive. Its marks are here in abundance: the leat cut by miners from the upper reaches of the Walla Brook to Moortown; the bronze-age field systems, broken down and disused, created by levering boulders to the edges and piling them up to make walls; the hut circles offering the ghosts of long forgotten domestic lives; the stone circle and the stone row still holding tight their meanings. The cattle and sheep and ponies are tended by men and women on horseback. The army lie in ditches and fire live rounds in an area marked by red flags. A television wildlife presenter takes his turn to walk for hours and then sit and watch: if the nest of the red-backed shrike is not guarded, the egg-collectors will come and they have helicopters.

There is not a soul in sight but it is crowded with signs, and with evidence of labour.

After a dozen strides the rhythm begins to knock me towards the trance, which will only arrive on its own terms. The body must be actively engaged but not challenged. A mysterious corner of the mind is then free to enter an enchanted state.

I will remain in this bowl of land for the next hour; I am running to its furthest edge.

To write this story, *What The Children Saw*, is my long, long run, the ground will be covered many times; it is always my aim to finish.

The pleasure in the work, and its difficulty, is not just to finish well enough, but to bring it to life, to make it capable of enchantment.

Kick and thud and kick and thud …

I have taken a wrong path; the faces of the book group told me even as I walked into the room. They smiled and talked with polite goodwill, but they were downcast. I have put them into a position where they must confess they do not like *What The Children Saw*. I had warned them it might happen. I had asked them to give only their unvarnished reaction. We do not know each other and there are only three of them; they like to keep the group small. They are all women. The work has failed them. And they will have been trying hard for me.

The usual greetings were quickly passed over and we sat down to hear their views. They, unlucky to have to do this, sat down wearing their normal human faces: the familiar nose, mouth, the pair of eyes, the forehead, all as they should be. But I sat at the table as Titania, I could lift my hands to my face and feel myself as the enraptured fairy queen, long hair decorated with garlands made from woven grasses. And my typescript, a block of white paper marshalled on the table, to me was the most lovely thing I had ever seen; I had wound myself around the work slowly, steadily, in the most loving way:

> So doth the woodbine the sweet honeysuckle
> Gently entwist; the female ivy so
> Enrings the baby fingers of the elm.
> O how I love thee! How I dote on thee! (IV.i.42-5)

Yet it wore the head of a donkey: ears as big as marrows and like cardboard to the touch, with fur growing inside. The jaw was long and bristling with hair especially from its lower parts. The eyes were large and docile on each side of the head. The mouth had that loose, affectionate slump of the bottom lip.

Titania, myself-as-writer, had swooned, blinded by love, unable to see what the others had seen and now told me was there: Bottom.

This situation did not have the carefree trickery of the Shakespeare play. It was not a comedy except insofar as it was an embarrassment, which is usually funny for someone standing at the correct distance from events — not too far, but not too close either — certainly not as close as where I was standing. When Puck loosens the drop into Titania's eye and she falls in love with whatever creature she first sees, it is a light-hearted trick: Titania is Puck's plaything and the object of Oberon's punishment. In my version, Puck can fold his arms. I am doing all the work. I have grown, i.e. written down, my own donkey's head. The drop that I had released into my own eye, and every morning I had replenish it as I had sat down to work, was distilled partly from vanity, self-love; let us not forget that the drop itself was taken from a flower that turned to purple (the colour of vanity) from milkwhite when it was accidentally struck by Cupid's arrow, which had missed its target.

One member of the book group wiped the table top with her finger tips. Another looked across to the other members, seeking support. The third member leaned forward and said, 'We didn't think it worked, really.' My last hope — that at least one of them had liked it — disappeared.

The words were soothing in that they were truthful. At the same time, the sentence made my blood run cold.

'It's so ... crowded with stuff,' said another, 'but we didn't really care about any of it.'

I almost do not know where I am. It has been another form of blindness, this trance that I have been in, while running. The pump action of heart, legs, arms — the backs and forths — has been like a pocket watch swinging gently on a chain in front of my eyes: hypnotic. I look up, and the horizon looms nearer than I would have thought. The hypnosis has allowed the landscape to slip past unseen. Time disappeared for a while. I am awake again, on the shoulder of Rippator. The track will lead me to this crossing of a nameless tributary to the Walla Brook which rises in Gallaven mire. The crossing is a thoroughfare: evidence of its business is offered by animal droppings and wheel tracks, but no other creature is here now. The water is cold and slides into my shoes like knives. I am through.

The track separates into different strands, uncertain over the soft ground adjacent to the mire. The eye seeks the heather, where the ground is firm, so I can avoid the pudding land, given away by the growth of rushes.

After some minutes I reach an enclave of near-flat ground, grassy and free of boulders, and protected by Wild Tor which rises 80 metres in a near-vertical bluff on its western side. There's no name written for this idyll on the map but it is called Wild Tor Well. Here the Gidleigh commoners pause in their march around the parish boundaries that they make every seven years and break out their picnics and perform various entertainments. The benign charm of this spot is exaggerated by its proximity to the inhospitable abruptness of the boulder-strewn cliff, and my foot-fall takes me across the spot where I have run three-legged races, sack races, egg and spoon races, with my own children jumping in seven year bites, from babies in back packs to children sharing rides on ponies to teenagers walking. Now it is silent and empty under the cool sky, and my runner's pace is steady as I attack the northern slope of Wild Tor. I will rise those 80 metres, toe by toe, kicking against the steepness of the path, until I reach the 530-metre contour that carries me along the top of the ridge. My breath quickens by a factor of two — double the amount of in-outs, real work — but it is automatic. I refuse to look for the view until I reach the summit.

This is the work, now: to find out what went wrong with *What The Children Saw*, to see it truthfully, to kick once more against the edifice, to climb, to see what gives ... to apply the antidote to my own eye, and see the donkey's head.

Professor David Lynn, editor of *The Kenyon Review*, gave a usefully prosaic clue — straight from the ever moving-forwards rock face of fiction-writing — on how to proceed if things go wrong: 'If it works, you're golden. If it doesn't, you'd better find out what you did wrong' (Lynn, 2009).

What The Children Saw is the story of a game: Megan, David and Ben bring back to life a dead grandparent by adding water to his ashes, which are kept in an urn in the sideboard. This comic zombie I have called Muddy Grandpa. Once he is up and running, together they enjoy an adventure on board a man o' war crewed by various different types of British woodland animal.

And yet, the alchemy, the mix, does not work ...

I kick my toe against the work again. I climb all over it. I thought I had made something lovely, but I had not. What had gone wrong? How can I see clearly? I blink, and consult my ingredients, and feel them between my fingers. The mixture is crowded, the ingredients are many and various, but it lies inert in the bowl. It does not work. It is not undergoing that transformation into gold that the writer-as-alchemist looks for. Why not? All that work has been wasted.

My toe digs into the path; I will work my way up this slope. The gradient is sharp. It feels precarious, as if I am clinging on. The path is as narrow as a sheep's footfall, and sometimes lies buried beneath hummocks. Up, up.

A recent memory floats to the surface: I am in the sitting room of my home. In my hand is a decorative wooden plate, mostly black, inlaid with shell, onyx, and other materials. I am looking for a position for this plate.

There is an ornamental table in the corner. It is in a rickety state now but was once very beautiful. It is made of black wood, inlaid with mother-of-pearl.

The two items are well suited, I think; they would live happily together. Both are flat, round, black in colour with inlaid decoration. I slide the plate onto the table, and with a satisfying click it drops into place.

'Doesn't go.' My wife whisks away the plate and replaces it with an unadorned, cream vase.

Suddenly, both are set off to better effect: the table displays its unique decoration, whereas the simplicity of the pale stoneware vase announces its height, its stature, its *lack* of adornment.

A realization dawns, now, as I run up Wild Tor. To put an extraordinary figure against an extraordinary background is effortful. The comment from the book group echoes in my ears, ' ... crowded with stuff.' The figure of Muddy Grandpa, and the man 'o war crewed by animals — each on its own is capable of being powerful, but together they agitate the surface too much. In their clamouring for the eye of the reader, they destroy each other. I could not have both in the same story. A colleague's signature phrase comes back to me, 'Try not to try too hard ... '

The man o' war crewed with animals will need a plain and ordinary occupant: a schoolboy wearing a school uniform. Whereas Muddy Grandpa will need an ordinary setting: at the table of a family meal, or working in a corner shop.

They cannot go together; one of them will have to be excised. It is a huge piece of work. It means I am bogged down.

Beneath my slow, slow feet the gradient lessens and my breath eases. A rewarding sight is impressed on whoever makes it up here: the slabs of naked rock on Wild Tor are like granite dinner plates made for giants, piled on top of each other. They look precariously balanced.

Would I really have to cut out Muddy Grandpa? He is half the charm of the book. The amount of work it would entail to remove him would be daunting.

A new, further horizon opens up: the centre of this northern part of Dartmoor — High Willhays, Cranmere Pool, Lints Tor, Fur Tor, Cut Hill. It is a triumph to be lifted so high. The damp air saws in the lungs, my legs are back and forth in longer strides now I am on the top.

To excise Muddy Grandpa means cutting the book in two, practically.

Martin Amis said the same thing in a television interview on BBC 2's *The Culture Show* (5 Feb 2010) when he was describing the genesis of *The Pregnant Widow* (2010) — he realized he was writing two books; they should occupy different covers.

I can feel the clash of that plate, when it was put on the table. And yet the simplicity of the vase was dead right …

I would later describe this decision to a writer friend and she replied, 'But that's common sense, why didn't you realize before?' A screenwriter friend emailed me the same question, 'How come you didn't *know*?'

Oberon tells Titania the truth when she comes to her senses, 'There lies your love' (IV.i.75), he says in a disparaging tone.

I could have kicked myself. 'How come these things to pass?' (IV.i.77). It is a case of the drop in the eye: the blindness made me unable to see my own material, I became enchanted to ill effect. This form of hypnotism caused Titania's swoon and mine, and it lasts until someone or something applies the antidote.

To run along the ridge is to experience a sense of elation, of success. It is a reliable pleasure, like a good meal.

I — Titania — love both these elements of the story: Muddy Grandpa and the man o' war crewed by woodland animals. Was it true, would I have to drag out one half of the story, and throttle it? And which element should I cut? I was in a state of some distress, faced with the donkey I had fallen in love with. How could it have happened?

The idea of Muddy Grandpa was born out of an incident in my kitchen. My son, aged five, with some difficulty lifted down from the window sill a terracotta urn, and asked what was inside it.

'Rousseau,' I replied. It was the name of my wife's mongrel, who had died the previous year.

'Rousseau?'

'Well, his ashes. When he died, he was cremated, and we keep the ashes so we remember him.' It seemed like a monstrous thing to do, suddenly.

'Oh.' He took off the lid and looked inside. There was an inner bag made of plastic which he unfolded. He poked the contents.

Our conversation turned to this customary treatment of the dead body: burning it in an oven until only bones are left, and then the bones are raked out and put in a cremulator, which grinds them up into granules.

My son related how a school teacher had told him that the human body is composed largely of water. We discussed the possibility that if we were to pour water on the ashes and let them stand for a while, Rousseau might come back to life, shake himself, and begin to nose around and look for food. He would be hungry after a year in the terracotta jar.

The conception of Muddy Grandpa was an intensely private experience, born out of circumstances peculiar — and very dear — to myself. It was an occasion that I was vaingloriously attached to. My son, our dog, a distinctive, imaginative moment, grew itself from that sketched out play script to this prose version of the birth of Muddy Grandpa:

> ... a small bubble lifted out of the surface of the ashes. The swell of this bubble was accompanied by an unsteady hissing noise. The bubble broke and fell back to nothing, and then as if it were a lazy habit and having nothing better to do it grew again, larger, and another one alongside it. The grey potion expanded a modest inch or two; a minute later the mixture lifted out of the confines of the plastic bag, and it might have been expected to pour down the sides of the urn but on the contrary as delicately and precisely as the bamboo stalks planted nearby it *lifted*, grew upwards and formed a leg, two legs, hips, ribcage, shoulders ... a skeleton. And then an extra tweak of sunlight found itself uninterrupted by cloud and slanted through the branches of the monkey-puzzle tree — and touched the white bones of the skeleton's ribcage. As if it sucked at this sunlight and drew from it all the nutrients it needed, muscles and sinews formed along Muddy Grandpa's bones, as quietly and as modestly as the primroses unfurling in clumps dotted here and there. The brain appeared like porridge swelling in the saucepan if you apply too much heat. The brown eyes grew like conkers in their sockets. His heart wobbled and thudded in its cave. The lungs expanded and contracted in a simple two-step dance behind the rib cage. The arteries and veins came slowly to life, narrow and intricate as stamens, coursing through every inch of Muddy Grandpa's body. He began to change colour: he flushed with all the pinks, reds and blues of human flesh and blood. He came alive.

There was another aspect to Muddy Grandpa's character that was born out of this private, beloved area of family. He came back from the dead and the Gough children loved him, but they were particularly sympathetic towards him because, through no fault of his own, he did not manage to develop fully. They had not poured on enough water. When they came back to discover him hiding under a blanket, they found that his skin had not grown to cover every part of his body:

> They went closer.
> 'Be brave,' said Emma and they held hands tightly.
> 'Gerr away,' said Muddy Grandpa.
> They couldn't see him, hidden in his blanket.

'It's all right,' said Emma. 'We don't mind what you look like.'

'Don come clother,' he said. 'Too horr-ble.'

'It's not horrible, you can't help it. We're here to help.' Emma touched his shoulder, and drew him round, and lifted away the blanket. She couldn't stop herself from taking a loud in-breath, because Muddy Grandpa suffered from ... It took all her nerve just to keep looking. Megan was right: he did resemble Emma's Human Body model. A section of his jaw was missing so it showed how his tongue went all the way down his throat. Only half his face had a covering of skin, so one eye sat in its socket as naked as a boiled egg.

'Are you Muddy Grandpa?' asked Emma. 'Who used to work on the allotment?'

I, Titania-as-writer, had loved Muddy Grandpa first because he was conceived during a conversation with my son about a much-loved family pet, but furthermore because he was based on a plastic model called 'The Human Body', which was one of my daughter's favourite toys when she was between five and ten years old. The warning signs are there: my life is valuable to me in a way that no reader can possibly reach. I was poised to try too hard, to push Muddy Grandpa too far.

Dartmoor is a giant sponge and its air is so heavily laden with moisture that, running through, it feels almost as if I am drinking it when I breathe it in, and I can scent its freight of peat (like the scent drifts from a glass of malt whisky), and heather, and bog. Each of my limbs works; the cantilevers extend and retract, the muscles tighten and let go.

The Human Body model stood inert, on a black plastic plinth, coloured pink as chewing gum. A section of his cranium could be lifted off, and a quarter section of his brain removed. His stomach opened on a hinge and neatly packed within were the stomach, lungs, heart, liver and kidneys. All of these could be removed separately, and the young paramedic-to-be could work out how they fitted back together. Long outgrown by my daughter, for a year this figure has stood on my desk, watchful, while his physical condition was borrowed and given to Muddy Grandpa.

> It was incredible to see the insides of his stomach moving, like a bunch
> of animals were in there having a pillow fight. His veins and arteries

throbbed with blood and his lungs popped up and down like balloons emptied and filled. She was speechless.

'And look, here's where I put the kidney back.' Emma pointed to where the kidneys were.

'There?'

'Yes. Touch one, if you like.'

Ben gingerly touched the kidney but it fell off and tumbled to the floor.

'Damn!' swore Emma. She went to pick it up but a Labrador dog barged in, knocked her off her feet and snapped up the kidney and ate it in two gulps. It stood there, apologetically wagging its tail. 'Goddd!' cried Emma, distraught. 'What did you do that for?'

'Sorry,' said the Labrador. 'My fault.'

'The Human Body' figure was given to my daughter as a birthday present. She would be tentative, opening gifts. The moment of un-wrapping held the promise of success but she was allergic to disap-pointment and so would hold back, dreading the gift might not live up to that moment of expectation. She would tease the paper off slowly in order to delay the possible failure. If the gift was dead right, the donor would be rewarded with silence; she would be unable to offer thanks, or say any words at all. If the gift was a failure, she would would quickly rush to hug and console whoever had given it to her with numerous expressions of thanks.

On her fifth birthday, she drew the wrapping paper back inch by inch. Inside was a plain white cardboard box. There was no illustra-tion to hint at what might be inside. She un-flipped the lid at one end and looked in. There was still no clue: she could see only cardboard. She looked around at everyone and then drew out this inner section.

And there he stood, on his truncated pink thighs with all the veins showing, his head turned to one side, all the workings of his trachea exposed. When she opened his ribcage, there were all the delights of his stomach and chest cavity. His eyeball was removable. With his mouth open, he looked as if permanently surprised.

She was speechless. She put him down. She shook her head just a half inch. Almost imperceptibly, she rocked back and forth. She looked at him with a peculiar concentration, as if she were watching beetles crawling through grass. With the point of one forefinger she touched him and leaned over to peer more closely. She picked him up and tried to coax him out of his housing, and I clipped the wires with a pair of scissors which released him. Not for a moment did she take her eyes off him. She gave not a word of thanks.

It was nearly as good a gift as the wheelchair we had bought for her from the recycling centre. When she had pulled the sheet off that, she had burst into tears.

It is no wonder that I was blind in my deployment of the character of Muddy Grandpa in the story: all the love for my children was carried over into the birth of the character, with that notion of his being born from my son's pouring of water on the dog's ashes, and his being built with the physical characteristics of my daughter's favourite toy. There was a great deal of love carried on his shoulders, and there is a powerful element of vanity in love, and the vain person falls in love hardest of all, because the outward view is at the same time directed inwards: the love of another is allied to the love of oneself.

Here lies the psychological complex that is at the heart of so much bad writing. And yet one needs the love of self, and the love of the other, to a great extent and in copious amounts, in order to write fiction. Fiction is an expression of vanity, but it fails unless it can untie this dangerous psychological knot — one might call it the Titania Complex — that prevents the writer from seeing accurately his or her own work.

The south-eastern slope of Wild Tor dips sharply and I am running down the other side of the 80 metres that I climbed a few minutes ago. All the pressure is on the knees and the fronts of the thighs. Each jump or stride stops me from falling, and there is the emergency fussing with the length of each footfall as I read the holes, the rocks, the tufts, the direction of the path, and judge the distances between obstacles fast enough. I risk injury to my ankles, knees, and in order to fend off bad luck I call for these accidents — dare them to arrive — because it is in their nature not to come if they are expected.

At the bottom I feel my own weight suddenly redouble, like when you take a lift and reach the ground floor. Faced with the upper reach of the Walla Brook, I pause briefly and splash through.

The Walla Brook has dug out a near straight line to here from its birth place under Whitehorse Hill. As the stream has cut its valley, the boulders dropped with it, crowding its bed, worn smooth. Its flow acts as a measurement of recent rainfall. I give a nod to the ghost of fourteen-year-old Charlotte Shaw who drowned in these waters while taking part in the 2007 Ten Tors expedition. To ford the crossing marks the halfway point of the run.

Now I must climb Watern Tor. My weight increases. It is back to kicking the slope with my toes, and feeling the strain in the calf muscles, and the lungs return to their double-time work rate. The moorland grasses underfoot are many different shades of green, and each blade is stiff and pointed, like swords. Many creatures have passed this way, the ground is littered with their spoors. It all blurs into one vision.

The figure of Muddy Grandpa is not the problem, in himself. It is only when he is joined to the adventure on the ship crewed by British woodland animals, that he falls apart. I bring to mind the decorative plate, on the inlaid table. It is that moment that I need to look at, the click as the plate is put down …

When Muddy Grandpa recovered consciousness he was not where he expected to be, under the branches of a monkey-puzzle with three new grandchildren in front of him, but instead somewhere different: lying on a hard wooden bench, alone. The first thing he saw was a painfully bright sky coming through a paned-glass window so he immediately shut one eye and struggled into a sitting position, blinking away, and tried to work out what on earth had happened. He was giddy and his balance was all wrong; it was inevitable he'd feel a bit woozy. He found himself in a small chamber or room, with a low ceiling and walls that he could easily reach in two or three strides in either direction. Although it was small, it was constructed — walls, ceiling, floor, everything — out of richly carved wood, so decorative and ornate that he immediately thought it wasn't real, and the next moment he glimpsed from the window a stretch of open sea, which told him that he must be on some kind of man o' war ...

My wife swoops past and lifts away the plate. 'Doesn't go,' she says.

So I have to take out Muddy Grandpa. It does not feel like a decision; it is something I already know. When I am not Titania in a swoon, I can see what must be done; and have always seen it.

The plate was taken off the table, and the vase that replaced it created a stronger effect, by far.

To kill off Muddy Grandpa was not among the book club's suggestions (they would not have asked for such radical surgery), but they applied that second drop to my eye, the antidote to the Titania Complex, which allowed me to see the work as if from the outside.

I wonder if other writers struggle with this aspect of writing; somehow I think many do not. I would have to be kept away from my own text for a year before I could develop immunity.

I imagine the effect it will have if I strangle Muddy Grandpa: it will be like pulling threads from a tapestry. With his removal, some bits will unravel, others hold up ...

I say this easily in just a line or two — I will cut him out — but it is to throw away a year's worth of thought and work. And I am proud of him; it will provoke grief. Am I killing off the right part of the book? Should I drop the ship crewed by woodland animals instead?

I swap the decisions, one for another, as I run up to Watern Tor: first I leave in Muddy Grandpa and take out the adventure on the ship crewed by woodland animals. Then, the other way around. Each element of the book fights against the other. Yet the bulk of the novel is the adventure on the ship, and to cut it, and keep Muddy Grandpa, is like losing the table to keep the plate. More pertinent is that I know my love for Muddy Grandpa is dangerous, flawed. He has to go.

I run down Manga Hill to the abandoned farmstead at Teignhead: a roofless, broken-down ruin where the fireplace stares emptily, cold and damp, and the hearth is made of grass. I carry the decision with me alongside Fernworthy Forest, over Shovel Down and up to Kestor. It is not a decision any more; it is a piece of work.

Without the drop in my eye, without Titania's swoon, I struggle to see clearly, through mists. Already I am grinding up new ingredients, building real and concrete things in the work … the story swerves.

The slope from Kestor down to the lane is easy. At the cattle grid Tarmac is underfoot for a hundred yards before I hive off to take the Mariners' Way and drop through the woods to Glassy Steps: the river crossing. Upstream the Walla Brook has combined with the North Teign to start the Teign proper, and the river has gathered depth and width, having picked up the water squeezed out of Batworthy and Scorhill. It takes fifteen strides to cross the wooden bridge, which thuds underfoot. Two more hills and I am home.

That evening I murder Muddy Grandpa. Once again a chunk of A4 paper, neatly dented by my thumb, is inserted regretfully into the pink-rimmed, painted metal bucket that serves as the waste for my most beautiful phrases and powerful ideas.

Except Muddy Grandpa is a zombie, of course, and cannot be killed. That boiled-egg eye swivels towards me and it sounds like an order, 'I can be the start of a different book.'

2. Swim (2 hours 17 minutes)

These are my favourite swimming trunks: red with charcoal sides, of a lycra-type material, comfortable and with little drag through the water. Their usual habitat is the river, or the pool where my son trains with his swimming club. Today they darken and disappear under the saltwater of the Mediterranean.

The water is chill only because my skin is super-heated. The salt content is high; it lifts you to the surface.

I am not thinking of the work yet; I am grateful to cool down and turn on my back to look at the beach, sparsely populated, my pile of clothes a lonely punctuation mark, and beyond it, the white-painted town climbing, with difficulty, the side of the mountain. When I turn on my front, it is to face away from the island, and head towards nothing but blue — the sea and the sky — except for a small island, some way off, with one solitary building on it. I am out of my depth but the buoyancy allows courage: I will swim as far as that island.

This breast-stroke will be of the long-distance kind. I shall not dip my head to breathe out through the water. I will fix on the island and keep it in my sights. In double armfuls, I pull the water past on each side, and then kick.

Once I am a hundred yards offshore the mass of the water makes itself felt: to contemplate its weight and depth on every side gives me a kind of all-round vertigo.

Pull, and kick ...

A thoughtless concentration is provoked by the automatic co-ordination, the instinct of the swim. There is silence, apart from the trivial disturbance caused by my progress through the water. This is my work: to reach, steadily, and pull the material behind me, to reach again, aiming for the end.

And the sound of my own voice is in my head, because not long ago I read the opening of *What The Children Saw*, out loud, to the person who is paid to sit there and listen. A children's story is often read out loud, and in any case it is a beneficial exercise. A text sounds in the reader's head, and to read out loud is one of the ways that writers can more quickly reach an objective viewpoint from which to judge the effect of their own work. My listener is paid not in money but in time, because I will do the same for her. My voice was deliberate, confident. I could sense the pull of the story, I could see in her expression that she was involved. The Easter eggs, the graveyard, the children determined to play a game ... Every now and again she murmured, 'This is good,' and then she said, 'This is lovely ... '

I was winning.

' ... but it's almost like it's *not* a children's story. Is it ... a story *about* children?'

There was a warning in her tone, but I thought that the text was about to become a children's story, proper: the Gough children were about to go through the page, so to speak, and they were going to start their game. They were under the monkey puzzle tree, and they were going to be transported to a ship on the high seas crewed by woodland animals. The journey would start with Ben Gough, the youngest, being carried off by a buzzard that swoops down from the branches of the tree:

Ben had wandered forward a few paces to look more closely at the buzzard. He turned to face the others and bent to tug down the hems of his trouser legs, to try and make them reach as far as his shoes.

'You guys,' he began, but even as he plucked again at the cuffs of his school uniform jersey and fold them back so they didn't hang down over his hands, at the same moment, from behind him, high above, the creature, the buzzard or whatever bird it was, laid all its feathers down, folded its wings and, head first, dropped through the branches as fast and silent as a stone.

Emma cried, 'Watch out!' but already the enormous bird had swooped. They could see its bright, glaring eye which blinked like a chicken's — the lid rolling from the bottom upwards — as its wings opened to stall its speed and its legs reached forwards ready for impact.

Ben didn't understand why his siblings and Megan looked so white and fearful, until a set of talons as large as scimitars gripped him and in one blow he was knocked to the ground.

'Don't worry,' called Ben. 'I'm all right, except my school uniform is going to get trashed.' The bird flapped, but couldn't lift Ben's weight; it only dragged him a few feet. 'It could have eaten me straightaway,' said Ben, lying on his side in the dirt, 'and the fact that it hasn't,' he added, 'means that it's probably going to take me to its nest and feed me to its young.'

The buzzard, flapping heavily, dragged him from under the beech tree, into open ground, while his brother and sister started forwards, but they were slow and uncertain, they didn't know what to do.

'Godd ... Ben, you all right?' asked Emma.

'Don't come too close,' said Ben. 'You'll only get pecked. It will get tired in a moment and let me go.'

But the buzzard didn't let him go — here it could open its wings more fully and it managed to lift his weight.

At one moment he was in the air, and then the next he was being trailed along the ground.

'We have to follow,' said Emma.

My listener became restless. 'So is *this* the start of the story?' she asked.

'Yes,'

She frowned. 'OK. But ... I've loved it until now, do we lose all that bit in the house, in the garden ... has it just gone?'

'No, we come back to that, we go in and out of the game.'

'Oh.'

'You'll see.'

It had disappointed her, and now the story had to win her again. But it would, because this was my favourite piece of narrative engineering: the story would slip back and forth between the game and real life, seamlessly. It was how I had observed my children playing: they would pile up cushions and drape them with blankets to create the cave, they would use an abandoned freezer as a coffin, they would turn a neighbour into an ogre, and at the same time they would run inside for lunch and gobble tea and visit their granny's house — swapping between the game world and the real world as fluently as otters move between sett and water while playing on the river bank.

John Masefield captured this duality in children's lives. During the first few pages of *The Box of Delights* (1935) a boy's ordinary trip home from school is populated by card sharps, detectives, a murderer who puts his victims through a mincing machine, and a man transmogrifying into a duchess underneath a railway seat.

But my listener was disappointed; there was no question.

I must swim further ... The sea assembles itself in fathoms beneath my feet, and in miles and miles of water to the north, south and east. Ahead, an outcrop lifting from the sea, is the island I am heading for: it is closer, and now I can make out the small white building. It is a church, no bigger than a garden shed but with a bell hanging, silent, in a cupola above the door. I stop and tread water for a while. The seawater feels callous — the sun, also. They do not care whether I make it or not.

I am not going to drown. I rest here, without effort. The water holds me as if I were wearing a lifejacket. I am not cold, not hungry. I will make it to the island, and I will lie in the sun to rest, and then I will swim back.

There is nothing to pull me down, except if I were to be wearing a long dress, which weighs heavily in the water. If my hair were long, and braided with heavy beads, and, let us say, if I am a creature of the air, like Titania, and cannot swim.

In the middle of a long swim through deep water, suspended over a vast depth, and with no one in earshot, and nothing but distance to hang onto, it is easy to panic. I am not Titania, hopelessly in love with a donkey.

If my story is a donkey, its fur is heavy with water, and it does not know how to do anything but thrash its four legs and turn in circles until it is tired out, and all that braying for help means it begins to lose energy …

I assert my swimming position, face the island, and stroke the water, and kick, and nose my way along the passage that my arms create for me. I will get there. I will reach the end.

My listener frowned and leaned back in her chair.

'What?' I asked.

'Nothing, carry on.'

I have read as far as page 40. The Gough children find themselves on a man o' war crewed by British woodland animals. They have seen the Queen who is in charge of the ship, and they have had to run for their lives and hide.

'A lot has happened,' I said hopefully.

'Yes.'

'And now it's time for the game to take a break. They go back to real life and find out where they really are, and how they're getting on.'

'I see. Where are they?'

'Well, Emma is hiding underneath the grand piano in the living room. And David's trying to talk to her about changing the game.'

'OK. Go on then. Read some more.'

> 'I *like* the man o' war, I do,' said David. It looked as if he were talking to the side of the grand piano. The truth was, he had ducked down to look at Emma who sat underneath, but the sight had disturbed him. Emma had her back against the wall and her knees cocked up any old how and her large white arms moved as she stroked Gormenghast. He stood up and the speech, which he'd rehearsed moments before, refused to come. 'I like the man o' war,' he said, instead.
>
> 'I'm glad you do,' came Emma's voice.

'It's just … ' began David.

'It will be fun,' said the voice.

'Yes. It will. But. Can we still have the weapons? I mean, maybe not all of them.'

'I'm afraid to say, we are unarmed,' said Emma.

'And what's happened to Ben?'

'Don't try and control *everything*,' said Emma. At the same time a muddy shoe appeared with a thump; David was looking down at Emma's disembodied leg.

'So, we'll have to find Ben?'

'Maybe Ben will have to find you. Rescue *you*. Who knows?'

'Look after him, won't you?'

'Of course.'

'You won't hurt him.'

'No, of course not. He'll have a great time.'

'He wants to change out of his school uniform.'

'Well, he can't. He was snatched and taken prisoner on a man o' war. And that's that.'

My listener sighed. She looked uncomfortable in her chair. Her morale was low. 'It's not working,' she said.

'Why not?' I was drowning.

She looked studious, clever. 'It's like, I was interested, at the beginning of the story, as a grown-up. I was interested in the children, I loved it, and I loved who they were, and what they were up to. But it didn't feel like it was a story for children. And then, when we went to the man o' war, I felt like a grown-up who'd been asked to play in a children's game, you know that awful feeling, oh God, I suppose I'd better kneel down and pretend to be interested, for their sakes … hope it doesn't last too long … and so on. I'm lost, I don't like what you're doing.'

'Perhaps you have to be a child, to read it.' I was trying to keep my head above water.

'I think if a child would like it, then so would I, because the child is still there in all of us, and I can recognize a story that a child would like. I don't think a child would like it, either.'

'Not like the back and forth, you mean?' I asked. My great love of this piece was exactly this back-and-forth. It was the scaffolding, it was how the thing was built. It was as fluent as the otter, surely, that ...

She shook her head. 'Doesn't work. Each one kills the other. It's not a children's adventure story, and it's not a book about how children play together. It's neither, and it isn't anything in between.'

'It has to be one thing or the other?'

'Think so.'

'Can't be both?'

'No.'

'But John Masefield ... ' I began, 'in *The Box of Delights* ... '

'John Masefield,' she replied, 'creates one fabric, one weave. He puts you in the mind of Kay, the boy, the whole time. He doesn't create two fabrics of text, and place them side by side, like you have done. He creates one fabric, inside the mind of Kay.'

Later, I would go back and look at *The Box of Delights*, and I saw what she meant. The stance, the position of the text, had a unity right from the start, and, significantly, that unity was located with one individual boy, Kay.

The story starts with his arrival at the station where he has to change trains, and he has lost his ticket, and he is worried that two men standing nearby are detectives — 'Probably those are two men from the Yard' (Masefield, 1935/2000: 2)

And if they are, reason tells him, they will almost certainly be chasing after someone. When Kay 'overhears' the two men, it is clear we have entered a fabricated world, as he imagines speech for the two characters:

> ... he's diddled us. He's simply not on the train. Here's the description sent: 'Travelling first class. In appearance like French cavalry colonel, with waxed moustaches, very smart and upright, height five feet eight, age about forty to forty-five.' He's hopped off the train where it slowed down somewhere; depend on it. (Masefield, 1935/2000: 3)

The tone of voice, the manner and delivery, tell us this is Kay's game. Kay goes further, and invents an action sequence for the two men:

'Asses that we are,' the other cried suddenly. 'Oh silly chumps and fat-heads ... Of course, he got under a seat in a first class carriage and he's been shunted out and away. Quick, quick ... we may get him yet in the shunting yard.' ... Now that the men were running, it seemed to Kay that some dogs, which he had not before noticed, were running with them. 'They are Alsation dogs,' he thought, 'but they seem thicker in the shoulder than most Alsations ... ' (Masefield, 1935/2000: 3)

My listener was right: I had made two texts, each written out in chunks, and I had alternated between them, whereas in *The Box of Delights* the real and the imaginary are woven together from the start. The 'robber tea' (Masefield, 1935/2000: 33) is ordinary life — 'some dark curtains were brought down and spread over the table and adjoining chairs, so as to make an inner cave ... ' (Masefield, 1935/2000: 33) — but a few lines later, the fantasy is woven in: '"Here is the Punch and Judy man," Kay said. "I'll fetch him in"' (Masefield, 1935/2000: 33).

Masefield's dual world is woven like a rope, the two strands continually entwined, whereas I have placed my two strands end to end, in sections. And more significantly, one strand is written for adults, the other for children.

It is a tricky business to get out of the water and onto dry land, because the island, when I reach it, is made of volcanic rock sharpened into knife-like ridges. There is no helpful beach; instead the shore is mined with globule-shaped, black anemones, their spines also murderously sharp. A white cross is painted on the shore, marking where a ledge offers a low step out of the water. It takes time, but I climb out and cover the ten yards which take me above the naked rock where I can find sparse, olive green vegetation to tread on.

I make my way up the slope and reach the chapel. The white-painted building reflects a blaze of sunlight; it is the width and height of a single garage.

The door is unlocked. Inside is a bunch of desiccated wild flowers, some stubs of thin candles stuck in a golden basin of sand, and a little apse at the far end divided from the naos, the body of the church, by a simple wooden screen. Half a dozen cheap copies of icons in wooden frames hang skew-whiff on the walls. The deities face outwards, their eyes large so as to be demanding; they give the sign of their apparent blessing, the thumb touching the third, ring finger, to demonstrate the Trinity. A broken candle-holder lingers at the foot of a brick-sized opening. A cobweb-strewn censer hangs from a hook set into the ceiling. Behind the screen, the apse is the size of a kitchen cupboard; in here will be placed any offerings, and candles will be burned.

I wander outside and close the door behind me. This would be a private family chapel, and it would have been tough to float the materials out to this uninhabited island and land them without a jetty, and then to haul the stone and the mortar over the razor-like rock strata, and drag it up here to the top. And yet the amount of dust and debris proved it was hardly used. I wonder about the family who had funded it, and how they had made enough money.

Outside there is a concrete apron, worn smooth, fronting the chapel. It is hot underfoot. I lie down to rest and warm myself before I swim back. An idea is brought to me from a conversation I had a long time ago: that love, when it has travelled a certain distance, becomes indistinguishable from faith: love of someone becomes a belief in someone. And yet Titania's belief in Bottom is misguided, and the beliefs of the family who have built this chapel are (in my view) misguided. And my great love for the way I have built the text of my book — which had hardened into a belief — turns out to have been misguided.

I lie on my back in the sun, a trespasser on a small uninhabited island given over to the ritual attached to a vainglorious belief. I am Titania, drying her long hair in the sun, believing what her eyes tell her to be true, but how can she know that her eyes see properly? Underneath everything, as solid and trustworthy as the concrete, is the always-changing performance of nature, as callous, and hard-hearted as the action of the sun and the water. We deceive ourselves, and we believe what we most want to hear.

Enchantment ... the drop in the eye means that Titania believes in a particular way, with her mind rather than her eyes. 'Love looks not with the eyes but with the mind; / And therefore is wing'd cupid painted blind' (I.i.237).

Jan Kott, in *Shakespeare Our Contemporary* (1964) finds in Miran-dola that it is this very blindness which makes up the ecstatic compo-nent of such love, 'Particularly famous was a paradox of Mirandola's, contained in his *Opera*: "*Ideo amor ab Orpheo sine oculis dicitur, quia est supra intellectum*"; Love is blind, because it is above intellect. The blindness gives fulfilment and ecstacy ... ' (Kott, 1974: 223).

It is the task of any novelist to create this enchantment, this 'seeing with the mind.' The novel is its own belief-system in the mind of the reader: that is its existence. A story offers an escape into a different life, a more potent one, often more troubled and beset by greater dif-ficulties and more cruel punishments, but offering more fabulous re-wards. There is a test that must be passed before we are allowed entry into this fictional domain — a test both for writer and for reader: it is the creation, by both of them, of a belief.

The author and the reader approach the text from opposite direc-tions, but the author has already been here for a much longer time. They arrive in that 'Borderland' described by Philip Pullman, which is also where all Hyde's culture-making trickster figures (Hermes, Mercury, the Coyote) are to be found, because 'They are the Lords of in-between' (Hyde, 2008: 6). Here the reader brings his or her contribution and the writer brings theirs. They must work together, one helping the other, to build that belief. The writer will already have shipped the materials, hauled them across razor-sharp stone, and raised the edifice, with all the corners square and the roof sound. In order to undertake this feat and complete it one must be in love with one's material, and believe in it. Otherwise, whatever one's motivation in writing, the work cannot be done.

But the work is for nothing unless readers can kneel and offer their imaginative power, their belief.

The intention governing religious stories, of course, is that the reader should never leave the state of enchantment. And such is our delirious love-affair with belief, once it is there, we do not want to.

I sunbathe for an hour. I have no towel, no spectacles, no book; with the chapel out of sight behind me, no objects separate me from the natural world apart from my swimming trunks and the comfort of the warm concrete. All that is of human kind is an hour's swim away, in that small pile of possessions that punctuate the shore line. I wish to lose all that is built out of vanity, and live only as a function of instinct: to eat, sleep, keep warm.

On all fours — to help spread my weight so the blades of rock are less painful — I go back down to the sea. I take my time with that first step into the water to make sure there are no anemones. It is a relief to launch off and hit the deep water immediately.

The return swim lacks the sense of adventure of the outward one. It is merely the way home. Yet, it has a quality of its own — the sense of having gone somewhere — the achieved journey. The all-round vertigo is quick to return, but is not as potent with the beach and the town of Skyros occupying two thirds of the horizon in this direction. I find my stroke.

I agreed with my listener that I should stop reading out loud. We had visited the borderland between reader and writer, after I had slaved over my building, and she had gone through the door; she had felt the beginnings of an enchantment and had started to believe, but the spell had broken — a wrong note had sounded. The light had begun to shine through broken roof tiles. The walls had crumbled and she had looked up to find she was somewhere she did not want to be — not a good feeling for either party. 'Titania wakes up and sees a boor with an ass's head by her side. She slept with him that night. But now it is daylight. She does not remember ever having desired him. She remembers nothing. She does not want to remember anything' (Kott, 1974: 234).

Even as I make paddles of my hands — fingers pressed together, slightly curved — and sweep armfuls of Mediterranean sea behind me, and kick it away, the the answer arrives. What is necessary — the technical challenge, the piece of alchemy that is needed — is not only to have the drop in one's own eye, but to drop the same liquid in the eye of one's readers. I have challenged Titania: do not be Oberon's victim, take control of the enchantment and yes, put the drop in your own eye, but also in your reader's eye. Become an author.

I swim back with a new sense of how the materials of story work, their alchemy, and how febrile is the magic that makes up narrative. Everything hangs on knife edges of belief and love. We must have the nerve to continue. We must be positioned right on the nerve. Wallace Stevens wrote 'One reads poetry with one's nerves' (Herbert and Hollis, 2000: 58) and I would go further and say and say one should *write* with one's nerves. And I ponder the difference between writing for children and for adults. A phrase from my literary agent, Clare Conville, comes to mind; she said, 'Nothing is too good for children.' They are a perfect readership; they believe quickly and with certainty. But they will not work to stay in Pullman's borderland. They bring less with them than adults, and if the spell begins to break they will not try and mend it, as adults will. They are gone. There is something of Nature, in their callousness.

I am faced with some choices: should I take a lesson from John Masefield and weave the fantasy and reality elements of my story together from the outset, or simply plump for the fantasy on its own?

The answer will depend on whether or not I want to be a painter of truth, or an entertainer of children. It would be a more truthful picture to weave the two together just as I have seen my children do in real life. The mimicry would be accurate and I would like to write it, but I am drawn to my underlying, more primitive motive: I want to capture children in a spell-binding adventure.

The staidly willing Dell laptop is set up on the terrace of an apartment looking out over the sea I have just swum through. I slide into the chair and prod the machine. I go through the text and remove the beginning fifteen pages, and all the material interspersed throughout the adventure story that takes the reader back to the real world. Block on, delete — one by one, the real-life sections of text are blocked out and then disappear. Save as: WTCS.3.

It is going to be all or nothing: an adventure on a man o' war, crewed by British woodland animals.

This is the most wretchedly, impossibly, bloody difficult book ever. It is like writing with treacle poured all over the keyboard, it is like trying to to wriggle out of an unfair parking fine, it is worse than filling in a tax return.

3. Drive (3 hours, 18 minutes)

The dashboard of the Nissan Micra, at night, lights up like a broken toy. The rev needle is stuck and the clock always reads half past two. When I switch on the lights, the full beam fails to work. I try and remember when I last checked the oil because there is a leak and I will blow the engine if I do not top it up regularly. The Audi, a *folie de grandeur*, is long gone because I have taken so long to write this book.

The drive from my place to the main road is a flight down tunnels made of trees with branches feathering overhead. It is black as ink outside the scope of the headlights and I look for the kite which, on occasions, flies ahead — Harry Potter style — as if escorting the car along the bottom of the valley. White shoulders of granite stare out of the walls and warn they might put more dents in the sides of the car. Greenery pours from the hedgerows that cover the old walls. A cat turns from the headlights and trots fast, makes its leap and disappears through a slot in the hedge. I can see the slant of its ears change to backwards, as the vehicle rolls behind it. A gate yawns open; the headlights wipe past. The Northmore Arms advertises its business using two words and an arrow written in white on a black slate poking out of the hedge, 'Good Pub'. The old beech tree grows tired in its patch of earth in the middle of the T-junction as I sweep left. A small window lets onto the roadside: it shows a glimpse of coloured bottles and the swing of the barmaid's flaxen hair. This sharp corner with its pub has the knack of gathering people like leaves in the elbow of a drain pipe: they drift out of the darkness in ones and twos and the more there are, the more they become stuck. They concentrate on one another, promote rivalries, commit seductions, carouse. This corner has a heat to it that disappears after the apex of the bend, as night reclaims the lane.

The road is staged with invisible memories: here I stuffed the Subaru into the front of that Jeep during the snow, on this curve I dinked the front end of the Mitsubishi, on this narrow bridge I pinched the front tyre between a granite stone and the wheel rim and burst it, in the middle of the night …

At the main road it is one left turn, one roundabout, a drift over a motorway bridge, and then up the slip road to join the dual carriage-way. The speedometer starts to vibrate at sixty and does not like to go any further. The white lines and the cats' eyes hold the car on its track. Music plays and the sense of comfort, of pleasure, makes itself felt. The state of hypnosis steals up. The body is actively engaged but switches to automatic, the mind concentrates on something it has done count-less times before and this provokes another part of the brain to come forward and occupy the mind's eye. The trance is found.

I am seeing an email string: a correspondence with my agent. Her words write themselves again, 'I'm with you all the way, until the first mutiny. There's something wrong at that point … '

But this is the point where the story takes off, surely? The Gough children are on the man o' war. The Queen, in charge of the ship and excited to have human company, has attempted to adopt the children as her own, but they have escaped, and have joined the Queen's rebel daughter, hiding away in the hold of the vessel. The arrival of the hu-man children is heralded by a basset hound, called Henry:

> The circle of lamplight moved with the children at its centre, and, before they'd taken many strides, its outer edge crept forwards to reveal an enormous, male basset hound reclined on a bed of sheep's wool and old cushions, and, as they watched, he dragged up his front end, lifted his deep, enormous chest, which was propped on a pair of stumpy front legs. His ears hung like curtains on either side of the heavy, noble face. His eyes, bloodshot, hung in a mess of goo after a sleep of so many months, and he blinked twice to try and clear them. The lower eyelids hung down low enough to fit a golf ball inside them, and the flaps of his jowls wobbled as if he were a species of reptile. His voice was deep, sonorous. 'Hnnnghh arggghh naaowww,' he said, yawning.
>
> A dozen starlings winged their way around the interior, the flock shaping itself into what looked like a single creature, twittering, 'Naooww.' They broke formation suddenly, like an exploding firework, and each headed in a different direction, twittering, 'Now, now!'
>
> 'Hold on,' Victoria shouted. 'He didn't say anything like that.'
>
> Henry slowly rolled backwards in his bed; he lay stretched out on his flank and his enormous head sank into the sheepskin. 'Now it's

time,' he murmured, before his eyes closed again, and he returned to his sleep.

'What's going on?' asked Emma. 'What's happening now?' But she couldn't hear herself speak such was the intense excitement at the basset hound's announcement.

The animals who had gathered around him fled — there was a rush outwards, and determined cries filled the air.

Victoria strode in every direction; she called, 'Wait! Come back!' Not one creature took any notice and so she called louder at the departing creatures, 'It's no good starting up any old how, just because the basset said so.'

'Starting up what?' asked Emma.

A mouse ran over Emma's foot. It squeaked repeatedly one word, 'Mutiny,' before it disappeared with a squirreling movement through a hole in the floor.

I loved this bit. The Gough children would react variously to the sudden, unprepared mutiny: the girl, Emma, would attempt to join in and help, while the boys would be afraid.

In the hallway of our home, in his green plastic dog bed (lined with sheepskin), lies our own basset hound, Henry. How could the basset hound be the problem? It was only a short sequence, and carried its own weight. How could my email correspondent object to the mutiny announced by the basset? The mutiny changed the story's gearing, accelerated the action, and provided incident, and colour. I untangled the email string, and more of her words came to me, 'It felt like you were throwing mud at the story, and hoping it would stick. It felt like you were bullying your characters. You point them first in one direction, and then in another, and you toss events in front of them, in their path, and then shove them forwards, through all this *stuff* you've thrown down for them … '

My mutiny, which I loved for its vitality, its invention, she had described as, well, *stuff*.

There was a pattern emerging within these three examples of potential cuts or changes. The first big cut I had made was the figure of Muddy Grandpa, and the Human Body, on which he was based, had been a much-loved figure in our home. The second big cut to the

---

Writing exercise no. 17: 'Murdering your darlings'

Read your own work, while trying to put yourself into the shoes of an ordinary reader. As you do so, make a list of those passages that you love the most.

Take these chosen passages and de-construct *why* it is that you love them so much. To what extent do they refer back to your own life, in some way? Are they passages where you think your phrase-making is particularly beautiful? Are they, therefore, dangerous? Are they indulgent? Give yourself the task of, in theory, cutting them out — face up to that possibility. Consider whether the story would be improved by taking them out or diminishing them. Consult your tame reader specifically about these sequences, and whether or not they work.

---

text had been the back and forth orchestration of the text, between the real world and the game world. I had loved this piece of narrative engineering because I had witnessed its real-life model happening in my own home, with my own children. A third cut, or change, now being suggested in this email correspondence with my agent, was this mutiny triggered by the basset; and, slumbering in our hallway is our own basset.

As Jan Kott pointed out, if it is love that creates the blindness, maybe it is also true to say the blindness creates the love, but in the case of a writer love is self-centred, it is love of one's own work, one's own reflection, so vanity is the uninvited guest. These threads — vanity, love, ambition and blindness — make the tangle, but it is effortful vanity on the one side and overweening ambition on the other that tightens the knot at the heart of The Titania Complex. I was trying too hard.

The inability to untie this knot is damning to the text, and the only way to untie it is to become our own reader, as if arriving from a distance, and to read carefully and draw it apart. In re-writing we need to bring to bear our skills as writer/alchemists: concentrating on the magic of our adaptive mimesis.

To fling down the mutiny and the basset hound and the man o' war in front of my characters meant that I had turned Emma, David and Ben into victims of the story, mere passive sufferers of my invention.

I have been like the army commander who tries to keep his troops awake for too long, who no sooner whips his platoon to one hilltop, before he enthusiastically turns them towards another, that they cannot quite see the point of reaching. I have issued this challenge to Titania: become an author, take charge of your army. Stay in your enchanted place — it is entirely necessary to do so — but enchant your reader also.

One car's length ahead, a lorry veers over the white lines in a drunken swoop before rolling back to safety. I grip the steering wheel harder and squeeze on the accelerator until the whole car is shaking and I burst the 70 mph barrier to crawl past him. It is like being in Apollo 13, except with wheels.

The white lines settle back into their lengths and gaps; the cats' eyes string out their beads for as far as the headlights reach. The music competes with the engine noise.

This mutiny …

I have fallen into a habit: I am relying on the eyes of other people — the Little Book Club, my listener, my email correspondent, my agent — not thinking I can trust my own eyes. As a result I am in danger of losing my way, of writing to different patterns cut and assembled by other people.

The trick must be, to use one's love, one's vanity, and that blindness, as the the wellspring of invention … after all, the trance-like state of writing fiction must be generated, in that very dark, blind, love-filled spot, surely? And then fill the pipette with that same liquid, and lean over the reader …

Alchemy allows for the creation of that drop, and for the lowering of it into the reader's eye.

Khaki green book covers enclose my copy of Oscar Wilde's letters. In here he describes how he spends the morning putting in one comma and the afternoon taking it out again. Another letter describes how he whiled away the afternoon, having to cut out the sequences he most loved.

I remember the late television dramatist Alan Plater, his expression heavily furrowed, the lines cut by his love of tobacco, drink and jazz music, in the living room of his Hampstead apartment. He said,

'Don't let me get up on my soapbox. For God's sake someone stop me writing about what I most care about, hmmm?'

I also remembered a performance I had seen of Ionesco's *The Chairs*. The opening night had aroused excitement in the audience: afterwards they had clustered around the star performer. His attack, his pace, had been just right. The inflexion had been perfect. The momentum (most of the dramatic power of the piece depends on a rising sense of hysteria) had built in waves that lifted and carried the audience at the right moments, for the right distances. The sense of his believing what was happening, himself, was fully realized. He imprinted us with this belief and carried all of us with him.

I saw it again on the following night. The performer had taken all the praise, the belief in him, and soaked his performance in it in order to make it better. Instead, it made everything worse: the piece slowed down with the weight of its own importance. He became self-conscious. Instead of living in the work, he was putting in front of us, for us to examine, his recently enhanced reputation. It was fatal to the flight of the piece. It was like watching a bird shot down. Something that had seemed impossibly beautiful on the previous evening had become ruined by effort. And yet it had all been done in our name, in an attempt to try hard for us.

These memories and thoughts have carried me for miles, there and back. Reversing the car into the garage, I check the side mirrors for the familiar markers that guide the Nissan into its slot. In the driver's mirror, it is the granite wall. In the passenger mirror, the stacked green trays that belong to the Tesco home-delivery service leave only an inch to spare. When I switch off the engine, sudden quietness invades the car.

I forget where I have been. For a moment it is pleasant, the sensation of having arrived home from nowhere, or from everywhere. By the time I elbow open the driver's door, it has become odd. Where *have* I just been?

It is dark outside. The lamps standing in the windows of the house make it look cheerful. I will go inside, into the warmth. As I walk across the yard I still have no idea from where I have returned.

5. THE CONSTANT GARDENER

1. The Yard

If the last analogy was about cutting stuff out, this final one, The Constant Gardener, concerns itself with what is missing. In other words, what might need to be planted in a novel to make it work better.

We have dug out the bank. The dumper truck carries a ton of earth in one go; the wheel steers the rear axle instead of the front, so its dance around the corners is odd. In the field, the spoil is dumped in heaps.

With each scoop of the digger's arm the bank of earth disappears. My son will no longer be able to jump out of his bedroom window; if we play kick-the-can he will have to use the stairs. He leans out and says, 'It's *so* far down … '

We are excavating a yard: this aspect of the house is a sun trap and we want a flat area to bump against the house, so we can catch it.

Wilf Hutchins chains boulders to the hoist, trundles them forward, and lowers them into position to make a retaining wall 8' high. It is die-straight, the faces of the stones as if planed by machine, the joints neat. The strength of the wall, its ability to hold back the hill, is in its extraordinary weight.

Sunlight will reach three corners of the yard at different times. At around ten in the morning, in the summer, the sun will choose first the corner where we have built the semi-circular granite steps which lead down into the yard. From then on, the area of sunlight will expand northward and eastward until it brightens three quarters of the yard. Around its edges we will grow wisteria, clematis, Apple Blossom, Ballerina, Autumn Joy.

The southern corner, sequestered in the 'L' shape made by the eight-foot wall and the house, will remain out of direct sunlight from dawn to dusk. The stone flags with which we have paved the rest of the yard are cut to leave a semi-circle to match the shape of the steps that descend its neighbouring corner. In this small patch that is shaped like a quarter of a cake, where there is plenty of daylight but no sun, and where the subsoil, at the moment, looks like a barren desert, we want to grow something.

I have in mind the words of Gertrude Jekyll, in her book *Colour in the Flower Garden,* 'Whether the arrangement is simple and modest, whether it is obvious or whether it is subtle, whether it is bold and gorgeous, the aim is always to use the plants to the best of one's means and intelligence so as to form pictures of living beauty' (Jekyll, 1995: 19).

There is a dark place — a hole, a gap — at the heart of my story. It is like this: the Gough children join a man o' war crewed by British woodland animals. They are seasick, and have very little food. Moreover, the Queen wishes to adopt them as her own.

Of course they want to escape, to get home: like Snow White, Hansel and Gretel, all 101 Dalmations, Dorothea, the Tin Man, Scarecrow and Lion. They all wanted to go home. And readers of these other stories wanted it for them; it became our passionate concern, as well as theirs, to see them safely back.

And yet, in my story, the reader does not feel this sense of objective. If I were to stand over the reader and ask him or her to think about it, to imagine their own doorstep, across which they must pass to reach their hearth, then I could perhaps persuade them they ought to be thus concerned and of course they will understand the children want to go home. But left to their own devices, with just the text, readers do not feel it in their bones, they do not live it. I previously described it as the heart of the story, but technically speaking it is the spine.

A novelist friend of mine, when I was describing this, immediately saw what the problem was. He said, 'It's because they're inside their own game.' It was like a door opening. He defined it more closely, 'We understand it is their choice to be in the game, and so the fact that they want to get home doesn't register, except in theory. This man o' war is their invention; they are only there because they want to be; therefore, the idea they might "want" to leave it and go home is meaningless, because they "want" to be in the game. The underlying truth is, they already are in their home.'

It was a fatal dichotomy at the heart of the logic. It did not matter if the children were hungry, or if the Queen forced them to do extra lessons in Maths and composition if, at the outset, this was a world of their own invention, in which they had chosen to remain?

'So there's literally no story,' said my novelist friend. 'However hungry they are and however much they organize a mutiny and so on, it doesn't matter.'

If I do not find something to grow in this barren spot, the overall design will fail. It is a curious feeling to have written a story that is missing its spine. To write is such a feral business: one must get one's hand's dirty, and yet move cleanly; one must celebrate all clever thoughts and at the same time forget one's intelligence; one must crawl through undergrowth and at the same time fly, and in terms of verbosity one must eat like a pig and at the same time starve, to write well. I had come out the other side not quite knowing what was in hand.

In our shady corner of the yard there is no topsoil; it has been carried away, along with dumper-loads of the subsoil and clutches of granite boulders, some of which — the ones with nice faces — have been used to build the wall. What is left is like coarse-grained sand, apricot in colour, peppered with stones and densely packed, devoid of organic matter. It has lain undisturbed by any root, or by any living thing, for thousands of years. It is not going to start being productive, generous or fertile, not without help.

Behind the house, no more than a short wheelbarrow ride distant, are three conical compost bins. The tops are shaped like Frisbees and are annoyingly difficult to open: the fit is too tight and they have to be kicked, or something-to-hand can be used to pry them off. There are no such irritations today: I merely lift the whole Dalek-shaped cone up in the air and put it to one side. The exposed pile of compost smokes with a density of miniature flies. I shovel the compost, load after load, into the wheelbarrow, and haul them around to that shady corner of the yard. The barren subsoil disappears underneath black, febrile cake which smells powerfully of death and decay, sustenance for life and growth. Every few days, as the compost lowers under its own weight and its goodness leaches into the soil, I add more.

This failure in the story, this rotten area, must be turned around; I must plant something strong enough to stand up for itself. And not only plant it, but grow it. The Gough children want to go home. I racked my brains as to how to elevate this objective to something that is felt, as an experience, for the reader, which he or she desires even more firmly than the characters. Either there would be something important to return home for — a fire in the hearth, a meal, a loved one — or there would be a dreadful penalty in staying. The carrot or the stick, or both. And yet, anything I might think of would not work. Since it is their game, they could break off and go home any time they wanted.

My novelist friend's voice crackled on the end of the phone. He has the habit of calling from expensive London restaurants. And now he gave me the answer. 'What about,' he suggested, 'if you make it so they're *trapped* in their own game? It all goes well, and they arrive in their game, but suddenly they *can't* go back?'

There it was as miraculous, as fast-growing, as buddleja, as sunflowers or Gunnera majestica. The story was suddenly full-size. It could be summed up in a few words: three children become trapped in their own game. It had vigour, energy. Already one wished for them to escape, and reach home.

Jonathan Franzen, in the *Guardian* (Review Section, 3 October 2010, p. 6), wrote about a gift that he received in a similar way from a writer friend. In his case he was given not the answer but only a hint, but it was sufficient to allow him to discover the answer for himself. He describes the writing of *The Corrections* (2001), in which the character Chip Lambert stands in for the author. The effectiveness of the story was compromised by the shame suffered by Chip Lambert and by Franzen himself. He gives an exciting list of subjects about which he felt ashamed:

> … of having married so early, ashamed of how strange and singular my marriage had been, ashamed of my guilt about it, ashamed of the years of moral contortions I'd undergone on my way to divorce, ashamed of my sexual inexperience, ashamed of what an outrageous and judgmental mother I had, ashamed of being a bleeding and un-defended person instead of a tower of remoteness and command and intellect like Don DeLillo or Pynchon, ashamed to be writing a book that seemed to want to turn on the question of whether an outrageous Midwestern mother will get one last Christmas at home with her family … I was mired in shame … Much of my shame became concentrated in the character of Chip Lambert.

And he identifies the problem that arises as a result. His main character, Chip Lambert —

> … became horribly repellent … every time I held my breath and produced a new batch of Chip pages, I ended up with stuff so icky it made me want to take a shower … There seemed to be simply no way to translate my singular weird experience into a more general and forgiving narrative that would delight the reader, rather than send the reader running to the shower.

Franzen walked around this problem for a year, considering it from every direction, with no result. The book was stillborn, the author not an author at all, let alone the famous one he was about to become. And then the answer came to him, the idea of what to plant, what to grow in that dark corner of the story, which would bring the novel to life, which would give the character of Chip Lambert to his readership in such a way that he would arouse pleasure rather than revulsion. He had the idea after a cryptic comment from a friend, the short-story writer David Means:

> He (David Means) said to me, on the subject of shame: 'You don't write through shame, you write around it.' I still couldn't tell you ex-

actly what he meant by these contrasting prepositions, but it was immediately clear to me that my task, with Chip Lambert, was to find some way to include shame in the narrative without being overcome by it; some way to isolate and quarantine shame as an object, ideally as an object of comedy, rather than letting it permeate and poison every sentence.

This was the clue that led him to a high-concept idea:

Chip Lambert, while having his dalliance with his student, *takes an illegal drug whose primary effect is to eliminate shame.*

This invention arrived in his mind accompanied by an immediate flash of recognition. It would be exactly the right thing, in the right place, if he could grow it successfully.

Once I had that idea, and could finally begin to laugh at shame, I wrote the rest of the Chip section in a few weeks and the rest of the novel in a year.

'Site Gunnera mamicata, for example, so that its immense, platter-like leaves tower over the jutting swords of Acorus calamus' (Brickell, 1992: 246). As gardeners, we are seeking the right shape, colour — the right experience for those we invite into our garden — and we will use all our powers to grow it successfully. One needs the same skill as the person seeking to position a decorative plate, or indeed a vase, so that it is set off to best effect. It is a question of taste and eye, and of course having the idea in the first place.

The Gunnera is an architectural plant, and mine was an architectural challenge: to plant and grow the way in which the children became trapped in, and then escape from, their own game. And I would aim to do so, 'With such thoughtful care and definite intention that they shall form part of a harmonious whole, and that successive portions, or in some cases even single details, shall show a series of pictures' (Jekyll, 1995: Introduction).

If the Gough children were to be stuck in their game, it would be necessary to think about the boundary between the game and real life, because here would be found a mechanism for preventing their movement between one and the other. Narnia has its wardrobe, Alice her rabbit hole, Harry Potter has his railway platform. These are portals between worlds, and I needed to have one now, in order to be able to shut it firmly in the faces of my characters.

Despite its being such a well-used symbol, I decided on the idea of a ring. If Ben wears the ring or holds it in his hand, he and his brother and sister can move into the game, and they can escape from it. The middle part — their being stuck — is simply his not having possession of the ring.

To grow this strand of the story, I had the following year-round list of gardening chores:

> Invent the ring
> Train the reader to understand its power
> Use the ring to enter the game
> Invent the loss of the ring
> And the searching for the ring
> Decide on the re-capture of the ring
> Compose the eventual escape using the ring

This constitutes an extensive amount of new material to be planted within the body of an existing text, so of paramount importance are the edges. Gertrude Jekyll, as she walks through her woodland, describes this with a wonderful bossiness when she instructs us how to cut grass pathways through woodland.

> [If the grass] is cut with a machine, then a man with a faghook must follow to cut away slantingly the hard edge of standing grass that is left on each side. For the track of the machine not only leaves the hard, unlovely edges, but also brings into the wood the incongruous sentiment of that discipline of trimness which belongs to the garden, and that, even there in its own place, is often overdone. (Jekyll, 1995: 31)

To grow Gunnera, create high humus content in the soil, dig in well-rotted animal compost, in April plant a single Gunnera bulb six inches below the surface of the soil, infuse soil every month with well rotted animal manure, watch for fast growth of succulent leaf stalks and fleshy, dark green lobed foliage.

It is not enough to plant new material without thinking how and why things grow, and whether or not that will deliver the desired effect. I will start to insert these new elements to the story, and sometimes it will go well. 'When the eye is trained to perceive pictorial effect, it is frequently struck by something — some combination of grouping, lighting and colour — that is seen to have that complete aspect of unity and beauty that to the artist's eye forms a picture' (Jekyll, 1995: 135).

The new beginning to my story must point the right way up, and it has to be planted close to the surface. This is the new opening to my book:

> Ben turned the ring over in his hand. It was heavy for such a small circle of metal. It was a yellowy-gold colour, like egg-yolk. Engraved on its surface was a pair of hands holding a golden heart. Above was a tiny, three-pointed crown, set with emeralds.

I must train the reader to understand the power of the ring; it is like teasing out the rootball so it is ready to grow. Ben Gough has the ring in his hand and runs into the garden to start a game on his own.

> ... and the ring lead him straightaway into the Forest. He rolled the boulder shut behind him. The ground was soft as a carpet. The trees grew more dense and branches scratched him. It quickly became dark. The roots snagged his feet and he fell ...
>
> It scared him to go into the game this suddenly, so completely. 'Stop the game,' he said out loud.
>
> His normal garden came back to him: the lawn was green, the fence wobbled along at the bottom of the garden, the old slide was there ... the broken skateboard. He was back, he was safe. He had visited a ski-slope, once, as part of curriculum extension week, and the skis had been safe enough when he'd faced across the slope, but as soon as he'd started to point the skis downhill, they'd moved off quickly and taken him faster whether he'd liked it or not. It had been a bit like that. Was it to do with the ring? He looked at it, lying innocently in his hand.

Some half-dozen or so pages later, I use the ring to enter the game fully. It is a question of making the space, giving it enough daylight but not too much sun. This is 'the planting of certain things that will follow in season of bloom and that can be trained to take each other's places' (Jekyll, 1995: 71).

When Ben is not alone, but instead in the company of his brother and sister, he is brave enough to let a game run on, and he uses the sudden rain during their picnic to imagine what it would be like if the rain did not stop, and the water kept on rising until it reached over their ankles, up to their knees, and then:

> They didn't know if it was the earth that dropped away, or if it was a wave that swelled and picked them up, but the water reached as far as Ben's stomach, and then up to his armpits ... He was the first to swim. He trod water, and hung on to his brother and sister.
>
> They didn't have the breath to talk; they trod water for all they were worth in order to stay up, to keep breathing. For Ben it was more difficult because he had to keep his fist clenched, to keep hold of the ring.
>
> The waves grew higher and the swell rolled more quickly ...

They are adrift on the ocean, and a man o' war drops its sails and slows to a dead stop so they can climb on board. They encounter the Queen who wishes to adopt them as her own children and they have to flee below decks. They have scared themselves and want to leave the game, escape. Ben goes to take the ring out of the secret pocket in his belt, and then he will be able to stop the game and take them home, but the ring is not there.

> A terrible falling sensation in his stomach made him sit down, and push his fingers further into the pocket to check — but the ring was gone.

They are stuck in the game. And now to escape they must search for the ring. This is the longest drift of the book. We have to protect our story, look after it. The idea has to be given enough food, manure dug in, and enough moisture, watering if necessary ... after the first frost, cut off leaf stems to the crown (beware prickly hairs on stems and leaves, which irritate the skin) and cover with a straw mulch ...

Where *is* the ring? The Queen has it, and she wears many rings. Each finger is crowded with them. Ben's elder brother, David, volunteers to be adopted by the Queen because it means he can get closer to her and look for it.

> All this time David's eyes followed the Queen's left hand like a dog that is about to have a ball thrown for it. He counted rings and he counted fingers. He watched for the trace of green, from the emeralds in the ring's crown.

I've never done such a major piece of planting before — putting in the spine to a story after it has been written. But Franzen's idea, too, was a major piece of architectural gardening. And the novelist Hisham Matar, with his award-winning first novel, *In The Country of Men* (2006) tells how he carried the book with him for a year or more, in London, in Paris, back to London again, staring at it, wondering why it did not work, until a big idea occurred to him and he gardened it in and watched the book come to life.

At the end of *What The Children Saw* it is Ben who makes the final leap for the ring, just as the gunpowder explodes and rips out the back of the ship:

> The flames coursed upwards, sizzling from one fragment of gunpowder to another and meeting not one speck of moisture. In a matter of seconds the flames had found their way through the deck above, and through the cloth sides of the gunpowder cartridges stored so carefully next to the stern-chaser cannon. Everything — all voices, all smoke and heat — was drowned in the explosion.

Now he has the ring in his possession, he can stop the game. He and his brother and sister are back in their picnic field. The summer rain has passed over and the sun shines. Ben returns the ring to his mother:

> Ben plucked up the courage and held out the ring. 'By the way,' he said. 'Borrowed this. Sorry.'
> 'Oh.'

He handed it over, and they watched as their mother strung it on the fourth finger of her left hand.

'Is it valuable?' asked Ben.

'No.'

The Gunnera is as big as a garden shed. It has an architectural quality: it is as big as a garden shed and it seems impossible that it has grown without my seeing it move. Rather like gorse, it has that sinister ability to creep up on you, fast. And there it is, in the corner of the yard, casting its shade-giving leaves. It is what I imagine a Triffid might have looked like. The size of the hairs on its stalks is remarkable. The green of its leaves is dark, luxurious — a plump colour. It guards its shady corner while the rest of the yard is covered in sunlight.

The yard has a table in the middle of it, surrounded by six chairs, set askew. There are two empty bottles of white wine that are a brilliant lime green in the sunlight. Four wine glasses stand, some with thimble-fulls of wine left in the bottom, others drained. The children's water beakers are clumsy and innocent compared to these tall-stemmed, drugged glasses. The dishes are done with; the forks are angled any old how. A few abandoned fragments of leaf are adrift on the walls of the salad bowl that my cousin gave us as a wedding gift.

The afternoon bides its time. I will read through some stuff.

2. The Small Garden

It is discomforting to find that I have written a novel and only on a third draft have I put into it the spine that it needed to stand up. But there it is: it is what happened.

I am lying in the Small Garden, a tiny plot around the back of the house. It catches the sun only for a few hours in the morning. It is seldom visited because it requires an extra effort to get in here: the walls fend off people and it is not on the way to anywhere else. The only reason one would duck through the gap is to be here. It has that air of places seldom visited: secretive, as if much has happened but all of it just missed. I love Gertrude Jekyll's description of what she calls her Hidden Garden:

Meanwhile the tree-empowered garden has a quiet charm of its own. It seems to delight in its character of a Hidden Garden, and in the pleasant surprise that its sudden discovery provokes. For between it and its owner there is always a pretty little play of pretending that there is no garden there, and of being much surprised and delighted at finding ... that there is one. (Jekyll, 1995: 58)

The greenhouse that stands to one side of The Small Garden has fallen into disrepair because the house was unoccupied for a while; the apple tree grew too close and its branches knocked against the glass panes. The guttering which once ran around the skirt of the roof lies in crooked lines, the supports rusted away; and rain water goes where it will. When it was in good order, this guttering channelled rainwater into a tank inside the greenhouse.

There was once a lawn that is now overgrown and dotted with patches of nettles. Each finger of growth from the box hedge has reached outwards as far as it can, competing with its neighbour to catch more light. The apple tree has yearly sent sprays of new growth in a southerly direction, and these new shoots have thickened. The tree looks windblown, with its arms waving in one direction, but in fact no wind stirs here, in the shelter of the house and protected by these overgrown hedges; reaching for the sun has shaped it.

I should be working but I am pleased to be distracted. I circle the greenhouse and disentangle the guttering. Much of it is useless and will end up in the 'Metals' container at the re-cycling centre. For safety's sake the broken glass panes should be teased out of the frames and replaced. I take a whole day to re-make the guttering, resentful that I have to use the grey plastic variety, which does not suit the Victorian style of the greenhouse.

At last it is done; now it can be used.

One shoulder of the house intrudes into The Small Garden: a right angle corner and a chimney breast made of granite in mottled varieties of grey with the odd splash of white as if seabirds nested in the eaves. A quince has climbed halfway up before its weight snapped the wires that had been arranged to hold it, and so it leans outwards in a constant, accidental fall, arms outstretched to save itself. A rotten window frame, crumbly and moist as pudding along its bottom struts, just about holds the glass in place. Through the window can be seen the table and chair, and the upright back of the Dell laptop, where I write. I remember the misguided bluetit attacking his reflection. The wallpaper on the Dell comes to mind: those soldiers, all staring at me; they know where they have to go, what they are supposed to do. But, the story lacks feeling. It is mechanical, as if I am telling its characters, go on, find this, get that, do this. So they do not feel much like doing it. This is the work, now: I have to plant and grow some feeling in the text.

It is clear which of the emotions I must evoke; this is an adventure story and it must secrete excitement. And that excitement should increase. In reading the book through, I can sense its lack, especially in the middle section. The story appears to wave its arms a lot: it is crowded, purposelessly chaotic. It is — in itself — excited, but it does not generate that feeling in the reader. And because I have failed my army of readers in this respect, it leaves them with the feeling that hundreds of different paragraphs — incidents — have been gathered up from somewhere and just dropped in this book, in a heap. And they have got up and run into the story any old how. Like The Small Garden, it feels abandoned and dysfunctional.

There are two story forms, or structures, which above all others generate excitement: the concept of a chase or race, and suspense.

I described in the third analogy, The Invasion, how David Mitchell generates excitement in the first and third sections of *Cloud Atlas*. Any writer has to work with the cold hard facts as to how the form of the race works best: it should be a close race, and it helps if there is an underdog who, we feel, must win, and it helps if there is some great cost attached to not winning. And it helps if there is, also, suspense. Mitchell demonstrated his engineering skill in these respects. He created a superb, rather pathetic underdog in the character of Adam Ewing; and, the race in the section of the novel titled *The Luisa Rey Mystery* could not have been closer. He lifted from real life the forms that most strongly invigorate our natural impulse towards excitement.

I propose to plant, and grow, a race, in my story. I can feel the awful cheesiness of it, waiting for me; a yobbish gang of clichés is about to spring up. The predictable manipulation, the narrative tiredness of all this. But, if we want to get the other side of it we must face up to the material and *invent* our way out of it. After all, the job of fiction is to invent, make it up.

The first thing is to think about the overall shape, and what goes where. It is not easy. Burckhardt uses Emily Dickinson to express the difficulty.

> There is a line by Emily Dickinson which catches, better than anything else I know, the essence of what we loosely call the 'creative experience,' which I take to mean the experience of anyone — artist, scientist, scholar, statesman, philosopher — who tries to create shapes truer than those existing. The line reads: 'After great pain a formal feeling comes.' What sets the great creators apart from ordinary men is not so much the capacity for inspiration, for vision — though of course these too play a part — as the ability to sustain, often for a long time and without letup, the pain of disorder. (Burckhardt, 1968: 12)

For the gardeners among us, the task is the same: the shape and size of the lawn, the creation of beds, the determination of height, and of colour, conceived with the notion of time, the seasons treading one on the heels of the next, always repeating.

I have decided that a round lawn should be at the centre of the Small Garden — a precisely round lawn. Because it is hidden, and because it is only ever visited for its own sake, the space has a mystical feel to it and a round lawn will create a mythical shape at its heart. Scorhill stone circle, not a mile distant from this garden, is testament to the power of the circle.

I uproot the nettles and other weeds and mow the grass. I then stand with a tent peg and a length of garden twine and a bag of plain white flour. Using the twine I determine the centre of The Small Garden. I like to be precise in this: just here the peg is pressed into the ground. A loop of garden twine is hooked over it. I unroll the twine to a length of fifteen foot: this is the radius of my circle and I am standing on its circumference. I snip the twine with scissors and tie this end around my middle finger. I crouch, and dip into bag of flour to take a handful: it is cool and soft as ... well, flour. I keep this hand an inch above the ground as I walk around and draw an exact circle. This describes the shape of the lawn. And then I attach another two foot to the length of the twine and draw a bigger circle. Between the two, in a series of four arcs, I will make flower beds, separated at the points of the compass by paths two foot wide that will form entrances to the lawn.

Along these white lines bites the spade, a mouthful at a time. Sods are lifted and turned. The barrow brings compost from the green bins.

The space is made; now it will have to be tended. The weeds will be removed and the grass kept mown.

To make the form of the race, in my story, I have to decide on who it is between, and for what. The three Gough children are prisoners in their own game, and the only way they can escape is to find the ring (it is a Claddagh ring). Therefore, if the race is to be run along the spine of the story, it can only be a race for the ring.

The logic is sound: if the ring has the power to allow people to escape from the man o' war, and the animal crew of the man o' war is enslaved by the Queen, then it follows that any among the enslaved animals would wish to have the ring and to escape, if they know of its power.

Which breed of animal should race against the children? A type of creature we can be made to dislike, but also admire, or even love ... My thoughts drift towards the landlady of the Northmore Arms who has a terrier called Sidney. This terrier attacks any other dog on sight — he performs this terrier-like, full-speed scuttle, barking and growling and baring his teeth all at once, until the lead snaps tight and the growling and barking is dramatically cut off as he is tossed in the air. He drops to his feet uttering a horrible choking noise but in two seconds he has recovered, whereupon he straightaway leans against the end of his lead again, his claws scrabbling against the Tarmac. When Sidney and my lurcher fought, I made the mistake of pulling my dog away, and much to his shame, in the excitement of the moment, my own dog turned and put one yellowing incisor neatly into my wrist, to the hilt.

A second terrier, up the road, killed sheep on the moor and had to be put down. A third attacked sheep, and, when he is out he has to go about wearing a harness and a lead, and when he is at home he wears a black box on his collar that gives him an electric shock if he tries to leave his garden. Terriers never give up: it is said that if their jaws close on another creature's flesh, they do not let go until the bottom row of teeth meets the top row. The only way to persuade a terrier to let go, apparently, is to insert something — a biro, or if nothing else is available, your finger — into its bottom. It must look around to see what on earth is going on, and forgets to bite.

A gang of terriers is going to hear about the power of the ring, and they will be determined to get it for themselves. They will be formidable opponents in the race.

So I must walk into the text — always taking out weeds, trimming here and there — and push it apart, create a space in order to plant this competition. It should start as soon as possible, when the terriers discover the power of the ring.

The closeness of the race is a question of varying the height of their achievements. If the chances of the terriers winning go up by an inch, the children's chances must also change, either up or down, but, whichever is the case, for maximum excitement they should at one time or another come close to each other — within a whisker.

The terriers might plant a spy in the Queen's quarters to keep track of the whereabouts of the ring; but then the children must either plant their own spy, or lose the one they have already planted. The terriers will manage to secure a firearm, but at the same time the children make enough serum for one poisoned dart …

The four semi-circular beds are planted. If I lie down in the middle of The Small Garden I can persuade myself that I can hear the plants growing. The effect I have wanted to create is one of seclusion, and also profusion. I want tall plants, a height of around three foot, so that if you lie or sit in the middle of the circular lawn, there is the feeling of a wall of plants and flowers around you. The height of the plants will be important. I would like them all to be within a few inches of each other, but not exactly the same — a little untidy. I want the the airiness and optimism that comes from a cottage garden offering tall, slender plants that seek the air, the sun, all crowded together, straining upwards. I have planted delphinium, lupins, campanula, white and apricot foxgloves, hollyhocks.

The solid earth against my back leads to the habitual thought — impossible to believe on this most still of days — that I am spinning, fast, in space. Moving at such a lick (without engines or any form of propulsion) that I will have travelled right around the earth by the same time tomorrow.

The form is 'both the anchor and the journey' ... Inside those few words of Heaney's lies the pleasure of writing fiction and poetry.

3. The Fruit Cage

Apple crumble is not as richly satisfying as *raspberry* and apple crumble. All three ingredients need to be attended to: the crumble should have oats included as well as flour, both for flavour and to bring chewiness; the apples should be prodded from the tree and peeled and parboiled immediately; the raspberries picked off the stems that afternoon and left unwashed.

I have the apples in plentiful supply. One apple tree grows next to the barn, the other stands on the periphery of The Small Garden. Sometimes it seems like the apples are full of intent: they crowd together on the branches and wait until we stray nearby and drop with a thump ...

But the raspberries I must grow from scratch. And I want the kind of fruit that itself desires to be grown, that almost throws itself at you, like in Andrew Marvell's 'Thoughts in a Garden',

> Ripe apples drop about my head;
> The luscious clusters of the vine
> Upon my mouth do crush their wine;
> The nectarine and curious peach
> Into my hands themselves do reach (Quiller-Couch, 1919: 39)

The area adjacent to the Small Garden already has rhubarb and gooseberries, and there is an oblong of ground here which has been invaded by couch grass. It will take some work, and I make a list: rotavate, wrap to kill weeds, build cage, dig in manure.

The pleasure in turning earth is doubled by the thought that I am murdering the couch grass. Some of nature's success stories should not be allowed too much success: the magpie, couch grass, grey squirrels. They are callous invaders like we are; their success is aggressive, punitive to other species.

I weigh down the black sheeting with stones, and watch as the plastic, during the weeks that follow, shrinks tighter to the earth, kills all that grows.

The fruit cage is built in two tiers: the posts and wire netting to waist height to keep out rabbits and the cats and then, above waist height, the green plastic netting is hung from eight higher posts, to keep off birds and insects. The door into the fruit cage is secured with a bolt. The door opens freely. To swing it back and forth, and slide the bolt home easily, gives me a satisfaction that I know will not last beyond a year or two: the post will tilt, the ground will snag the gate, the bolt will not slide home without the gate being lifted.

Manure comes from my neighbour's stable yard: as many bags as I care to fill, working from the back of the heap, where it is already three-years old.

For the raspberry plants themselves, I drive the short distance to Sooz's garden. There is a new bench positioned to face the view; a freshly-dug, kidney-shaped border breaks up the journey from one end of the garden to the other; there are blue-flowering, ground-hugging plants which I have never seen before. A swing has been attached to the oak branch that lowers grandly over the lawn.

At the bottom of her garden is the patch given over to vegetables and fruit, and I can uproot the stems that have escaped from her raspberry plantation to hide in the surrounding banks. There is something modest about a raspberry stem — weedy and nerdish, but offering this most rich of summer and autumn fruits: the soft glove, of a pale, blood red, that so gently drifts apart from the green conical stamen.

These stems have self-seeded, and it is like gathering an errant flock. We upend them, lay them on a tarpaulin and carry them to the car. After a short journey I walk them straight to their new home inside the fruit cage. I stand them up, press in the earth around their roots, tie each stem to a bamboo cane. They look forlorn, regimented like this. They have work to do.

In *What The Children Saw* I have aimed to achieve a suspenseful form, but one element is weak, it has failed to flourish. If Hitchcock defined suspense as a ticking bomb hidden under the table, then however much I listen I cannot hear the sound of ticking.

This time element is equivalent to the 'chuff, chuff, chuff,' of the train as it comes around the corner, its driver oblivious to the maiden tied to the tracks just a short distance ahead.

It is the cigarette burning between the fingers of Tippi Hedren as she looks the wrong way while sitting on the bench outside the children's playground in Hitchcock's *The Birds*.

It is the step-by-step descent of the new Mrs de Winter down the stairs to attend the ball at Manderley, wearing the same dress as the old Mrs de Winter, in du Maurier's *Rebecca*. The stairs are the clock: there is an inevitable tightening of the situation, as impossible to reverse as the passing of time itself.

It is the circular staircase which the detective has to run up in Frederick Forsyth's *The Day of The Jackal*, when the un-named assassin sights his cross hairs on the left temple of Charles de Gaulle.

I have the dangerous penalty, the 'bomb' part of the suspense: the Claddagh ring will be melted down to make gold ingots unless the children can get it back.

I have the 'hidden under the table' part: those who possess the ring (the Queen and her officers on board the man o' war) have no idea of its power and so carry on regardless.

But the ticking part — a deadline that closes, tightens the suspense — is lacking. There is no specific time set for the occasion when the ring will be melted down, when it will be lost to them forever.

How can I plant into the text a time element, to engineer the suspense form?

This is how the story works: the man o' war gathers gold; that is its purpose. The gold is collected by magpies who fly over nearby land masses and steal anything shiny from a milk bottle top to a torn-off corner of the foil which wraps a chocolate bar. The magpies drop what

---

Writing exercise no. 18: 'How to finish your novel'

It can be daunting, especially if you've not done it before, to write to a length of 70,000 words or more. One way of overcoming the magnitude of this piece of work is to cut it into a series of smaller pieces, and finish them, one at a time. In this way there is always a finishing line close at hand.

---

they have found on the deck of the ship and the real gold is separated and taken down to the Engine Room. In here is a forge that melts the gold and pours it into a mould, to form an ingot.

If the Gough children do not get their ring back, it will be tossed in with the other gold items and melted down. They will be stuck on board the man o' war forever.

The Queen and her officers have no knowledge of the power of the ring, and the children must keep it that way. If she knows, the Queen will use the ring for her own ends.

But I need to create the remorseless march of time towards the point of the explosion. The form, if it is going to achieve its most powerful effect, demands it.

Perhaps the melting down of the scrap gold could take place at a set time every week, or month? To test the idea it is necessary to go through to the other side of the page and live in the imaginary world one has created. There are various strands of story — 'drifts' Gertrude Jekyll calls her different areas of planting — that require that we breathe them in, experience them for real.

If I live in the world of the Queen's court, and it is my job to carry the scrap gold down to the Engine Room, make a pile of it, fire up the forge with coals and make it red hot, pile up the scrap gold, watch over it until it is molten, to pour, and watch it fill the mould and form a gold ingot, then to lift it away from the heat and allow the gold ingot to cool, lever it out of the mould, stack it with the others … does the logic tell me that this should be done every two weeks, or three … Is there any possible time constraint in this process? I cannot feel around for any reason there should be a set time, or a prescribed day.

Instead, logic demands there has to be a certain *weight* of gold before the crucible can be filled. A gold bar weighs 400 Troy Ounces. So this will be my clock — the number will be called out, from three hundred, to three hundred and fifty, to three hundred and seventy Troy Ounces ... When the figure of 400 is struck, the forge will be lit and the gold will be melted. The escalation of this figure will give us the sense of inevitable progression towards a definite moment in time.

In August the raspberries are ready to pick. The door of the fruit cage opens easily, still. The sun is low in the east and beats against my crown. The stalks bow gracefully under the weight of their dusky pink fruit, which always remind me of insects' eyes. I take only the perfectly ripe ones; as I touch with my thumb and forefingers the rear ends of the fruit bulbs they spring from the stem and jump into my hand, and tickle my palm as they run into the glass bowl. I am reminded again of the Andrew Marvell poem — the raspberries *Into my hands themselves do reach* — and it is this willing optimism I love.

The couch grass is coming back already. I will have to weed the raspberry beds. I will stalk the borders and rip out the ground elder, again, and the bindweed. I will cut out the Shepherd's Purse, burn the thistles, dig out the docks. I am always trimming, cutting out, pulling up, digging out, burning. The dandelions seed themselves promiscuously. It is constant work. One develops an eye for what needs to be there, and what needs to be cut.

Over a period of several weeks I occasionally place the glass bowl in the crook of my arm and collect more raspberries; and when it comes to the very last raspberry in this year of bonus fruits, I remember a gardener I used to work for, Albert, who, as he would make the last snip of the box hedge, or just before he would lift the last shovel full of compost, or as he would gather the last windfall or plant the final one in a row of broad beans, would cry out as if a touch annoyed, 'This here's the bastard we've been looking for all along.'

Appendix

Carol Shields and *The Stone Diaries*

I initially wrote too much about *The Stone Diaries* in the main body of this text but, in cutting out certain sequences, I could not resist including them in this appendix for those who might be interested.

In the analogy called The Invasion I talked about how authority and integrity are the significant qualities without which a writer's voice will fail; and those two qualities are partly proven by the writer's knowledge — or apparent knowledge — of the terrain that he or she proposes to take us across.

Knowledge of the terrain is made apparent at every turn in *The Stone Diaries* by use of specific detail and intelligent analysis. In seeking to make this point — believing the text to be steeped in this quality — I decided to open the book at random, and find an example. I found myself on page 68. Carol Shields describes the new legislative building they are constructing in the city of Winnipeg in 1916. 'Ground was broken in the year 1913' (Shields, 1993/2008: 68). This prosaic sentence is accurate not only in terms of apparent depth of knowledge (the actual year any building in Winnipeg was commenced), but also, it is imbued with authority due to its choice of terminology: 'ground was broken' is an architectural/construction phrase such as might be used by the project manager at a meeting of investors and planners, and therefore our trust in the author is increased to a greater degree than if she had merely said, 'Building work started in 1913'. She knows the exact type of stone used for the building — Tyndall stone — and she makes a sweeping analysis: the construction of this building kept the Tyndall quarry busy and therefore its workers (among them Cuyler) were not sent to fight the Kaiser. She has the micro-view (the name of the stone, the terminology) and the macroscopic view: the effects of construction on the local population. In this way, with a mixture of apparent precision and accuracy, she proves herself mistress of the territory and commands our respect and allegiance. The building might not exist, the name of the stone might be fictional, but the text speaks of her knowledge — even if it is fictional — of the ground she's covering. The tone of authority is perfectly judged.

As it happens, she is using this apparently ordinary, factual description of Winnipeg to site properly in our minds the extraordinary, fictional tower that Cuyler has built with his bare hands, stone by stone. The fantastic creation therefore borrows from, is attached to, is proven by, the detailed, historical reality (even if it is made up) of its painted background. We are in safe hands. We advance. Our morale is high.

And yet Carol Shields plays with the narrative voice in *The Stone Diaries* in a way that seems deliberately to undermine authority and integrity. She lies all the time. The photographs inserted in the book are false. Shields and her designated first-person narrator, the presumed writer of this *faux* autobiography, Daisy, play havoc with the readers' perceptions. When Daisy falls ill with measles, Carol Shields slips in and out of the point of view, in and out of different tenses, with deliberate recklessness. First of all, she (Daisy) describes herself as being ill from the outside, as if describing someone else, 'The disease went wafting through Daisy's respiratory passages' (Shields, 1993/2008: 74) ... and then without even a blink or a pause she describes the illness from the inside, admitting that she is describing herself, 'Well, you might say, it was doubtless the fever that disoriented me, and it is true that I suffered strange delusions in that dark place, and that my swollen eyes in the twilight room invited frightening visions' (Shields, 1993/2008: 75). Whereupon, right in front of our very eyes, she changes straight back again, 'The long days of isolation, of silence, the torment of boredom — all these pressed down on me, on young Daisy Goodwill and emptied her out. Her autobiography, if such a thing were imaginable, would be, if such a thing were ever to be written, an assemblage of dark voids and unbridgeable gaps' (Shields, 1993/2008: 75).

This playfulness in the working of the text recurs frequently. Daisy says, 'The doctor — whom I'm unable, or unwilling, to supply with a name' (Shields, 1993/2008: 74) — and so on. 'Her autobiography, if such a thing were imaginable' (Shields, 1993/2008: 74) — we are reading it, it *has* been imagined ... it is here, in our hands. But it is fake. It is a deliberate attempt to create in us a certain amount of narrative confusion.

On the bottom of page 76 we have this extraordinary admission by Carol Shields of what she is doing:

> She understood that if she was going to have to hold onto her life at all, she would have to rescue it by a primary act of imagination, supplementing, modifying, summoning up the necessary connections, conjuring the pastoral or heroic or whatever, even dreaming a limestone tower into existence, getting the details wrong occasionally, exaggerating or lying outright, inventing letters or conversations of impossible gentility, or casting conjecture in a pretty light. (Shields, 1993/2008: 76)

Carol Shields admits that she's confabulating this book, making some of it up and using other bits that are apparently true, in order to create the whole.

Surely this means her voice lacks authority, lacks integrity?

It has, ironically, the opposite effect — it creates enormous trust, and pleasure. It is equivalent to the television entertainer Derren Brown showing us how he has created his illusions. It is the equivalent of the dramatist Bertolt Brecht informing his audience — via actors who simply tell the audience — that they, the audience, must stand back, and realize that what happens on his stage is a deliberate falsehood, from which they are invited to draw their own conclusions.

Carol Shields creates the illusion, at the same time as showing us how she does it. It is a deliberate tactic by an experienced and high-achieving story-teller (*The Stone Diaries* won a Pullitzer).

Shields is an experienced commander of an army of specialist readers. She recruits the trust of the army, and has them follow, simply by telling them the unvarnished truth. A truth that they are not normally privy to, and which, by-the-by, demonstrates all her knowledge and skill in the art of writing fiction. The army will now march to the ends of the earth, because they trust and believe in the person who leads them.

So, just as Mark Haddon created an unreliable narrator in such a way as to create more trust, so does Carol Shields. I would submit that, in every sense, in these capable writers' hands, the apparent subversion of these two qualities in an unreliable narrator in effect breeds a stronger version of authority and integrity, refreshed by its strangeness. It is another way of doing the same thing: leading men and women across the ground that must be covered, and in so doing, to grant them victory.

It is also, incidentally, one way in which Carol Shields avoids the pitfalls of the first person narrator while enjoying all its advantages.

The Stone Diaries is a literary novel; it is conceived as a *faux*-biography so the overall objective is the telling of a life, which by its very nature will not subscribe to a single, linear objective. And Carol Shields is writing as a painter and as a musician; her first concern is not so much to entertain a huge audience from every walk of life but to achieve high-end, literary glory.

Nonetheless, forward progression — traction — is created with great subtlety throughout, in order to inspire her more elite troop of readers. Lacking the single, overall objective she deploys a series of smaller objectives, one after another, that serve the same purpose.

In the first section of the book, *1905, BIRTH*, Carol Shields uses dramatic irony to create this sense of an objective: there is something that we know, that the characters do not know. A wish is created in us, the readers, to reach the point where the characters find out. And, from our God-like position we can enjoy their reaction. That first section has us, at the end of it, standing victorious, our flag stuck in the ground, ready to move on.

In the following section, she does the very opposite. We are suddenly confronted by a new lot of Fletts. We recognize the name, but what is the connection between this Flett and the Fletts we met before, who were neighbours to Mercy and Cuyler, and witnesses to the birth of the infant narrator? Where am I? When is this? Who is Barker Flett? Why are we with him? I thought this was a book about Daisy? Where's Daisy?

A few pages later we receive the answer, and it is delivered with that mock-innocent, knowing tone of voice, because Carol Shields realizes fully that she has been tempting us towards this answer, and it is our reward; this is the bit we have been waiting for: 'Have I said that Clarentine Flett deserted her husband Magnus in the year 1905? Have I mentioned that she took with her the small infant who was in her charge, the young child of Mercy Goodwill, her neighbour who had died while giving birth' (Shields, 1993/2008: 47)?

There she is — the infant Daisy was adopted by her next door neighbour, Mrs Clarentine Flett.

With this answer given to us, Shields is sufficiently alert to recognize that she must quickly make a new objective, or risk losing our attention. She does so a few pages later, in the letter on page 53, 'We were most interested to read of your tower in last week's Tribune' (Shields, 1993/2008: 53).

What tower? Suddenly there is this small movement, or change, and our curiosity swoops — what *is* this tower? A few pages on, we are again told the answer — and our curiosity is satisfied. The tower is Cuyler's memorial to his dead wife. We still want to know more about it, and eventually we do find out how it was built and why.

And again, Shields is aware that she has created this curiosity in us to know about the tower, to understand it, because she has the courtesy to deliver us, her troops, to this answer she has stored up for us, full-tilt. 'Across the low-flying fields the tower can easily be spotted. "There it is," someone will shout …. Always, one or two of these young people will break into a run. "*First man there is a starving bear*"' (Shields, 1993/2008: 70).

The novel progresses in this way, as a series of small-scale movements. The reader is catapulted a certain distance into the future, and the changes, the differences, are felt in a visceral way because the logic that would explain the changed circumstances is, for a short while, absent, and we crave that logic, the question of how we got here. Within a more or less few pages the answer is given, and the next movement is immediately deployed.

Carol Shields starts small, but once she has trained us in the effect, she deploys larger movements. For instance at the outset of the section titled MARRIAGE, 1927 (on page 79) suddenly Daisy is getting married and we do not know to whom. The last time we saw her, she was a child recovering from being ill, and she was meeting her real father for the first time. Our curiosity is alerted, we aim our concentration at the story. To whom is she getting married? And she is a graduate of Tudor Hall — what did she study? And who are all these people?

Shields is so confident in this technique that she deliberately mucks it up. She pushes it too far and what is more, she tells us she has done so. Mr Cuyler Goodwill suddenly, dramatically, develops a 'silver-tongue' (Shields, 1993/2008: 83) and is a partner in the firm of Lapiscan International, which quarries limestone. The last time we met him, he was a maudlin, repressed stone-cutter building a tower in memory of his dead wife. He hardly said a word. How did he become silver-tongued? The story knows, but we do not. It is the amount of change that excites us, the degree of change, which magnifies our curiosity, and therefore increases the desire to concentrate, go forwards.

We get an example of Cuyler's new silver tongue in an astonishing speech on page 80, which summons the deep past, three hundred million years ago.

> Time ... teams up with that funny old fellow, chance, to give birth to a whole lot of miracles. It was, after all ... the lucky presence of a warm, clear and shallow sea, some three hundred million years ago, only think of it, my friends — that combination produced the remarkable Indiana limestone which has served all of us here so well. (Shields, 1993/2008: 80)

It makes for an unbelievable transformation in Cuyler. And she asks the question herself, in a knowing way: 'That silver tongue — how was it acquired? The question — would anyone disagree — holds a certain impertinence, since all of us begin our lives bereft of language'

(Shields, 1993/2008: 83). This is illogical, but she goes on to answer the question anyway and gives a ridiculous, playful answer. A stone in his throat became dislodged while he was having sex with his wife. She is teasing us, because on page 115 this 'silver tongue' is revealed for what it is — nonsense. Cuyler being, in fact, in Daisy's view, 'a bantam upstart, pompous, hollow. How does such spoilage occur? She knows the answer. Misconnection. Mishearing' (Shields, 1993/2008: 115). In other words, none of it was true. The writing itself becomes a game of logic.

Carol Shields, in one of the many narrative feints in this novel, is ticking us off for believing in the enormity of the change she wrought in Cuyler. Yet, there was no doubt that that speech about the ancient limestone was brilliant ... because it was hers, not his. But we will follow Carol Shields anywhere. She makes for us that movement in the grass that attracts our eye, and creates our swoop on the text.

Works Cited

Austen, Jane (1818/1934) *Northanger Abbey*. London: JM Dent and Sons.

Bacon, Francis (1905) *The Philosophical Works of Francis Bacon*. London: George Routledge and Sons.

Barry, Kevin (2007) 'Atlantic City', in *There Are Little Kingdoms*. Dublin: The Stinging Eye Press.

Barry, Sebastian (2008) *The Secret Scripture*. London: Faber and Faber.

Brickell, Christopher (ed.) (1992) *Encyclopaedia of Gardening*. London: Dorling Kindersley.

Brontë, Emily (1847) *Wuthering Heights*. Stratford-on-Avon: The Shakespeare Head Press.

Burckhardt, Sigurd (1968) *Shakespearean Meanings*. Princeton, NJ: Princeton University Press.

Byatt, Antonia (ed.) (1998) *The Oxford Book of Short Stories*. Oxford: Oxford University Press.

Capote, Truman (1958/1961) *Breakfast At Tiffany's*. London: Penguin Books.

Chabon, Michael (2010) *Reading and Writing Along The Borderlands*. London: Fourth Estate.

Cosslett, Tess (2006) *Talking Animals In British Children's Fiction, 1786-1914*. Aldershot: Ashgate Publishing.

De Nova Villa, Arnoldus (1611) 'A Chymicall treatise of the Ancient and highly illuminated Philosopher, Devine and Physitian, Arnoldus de Nova Villa who lived 400 years agoe, never seene in print before, but now by a Lover of the Spagyrick art made publick for the use of Learners Transcribed by Hereward Tilton from Bodleian Library, MS Ashmole 1415', 130–46, accessed June 2010, http://www.alchemylab.com

Downing, Judith (2008) 'The Grandmother Cycle', in *The Stone Diaries*. London: Harper Perennial.

Feaver, Jane (2009) *Love Me Tender*. London: Vintage.

Ford, Ford Madox (1915/2008) *The Good Soldier*. Oxford: Oxford Paperbacks.

Forster, Edward M. (1925) *Anonymity*. London: The Hogarth Press.

Forster, Edward M. (1962) *Aspects of The Novel*. London: Pelican Books.

Franzen, Jonathan (2001/2009) *The Corrections*. London: Fourth Estate.

Gibbons, Dave and Moore, Alan (1986) *Watchmen*. New York: DC Comics.

Glenny, Misha (2008/2009) *McMafia*. London: Vintage.

Goethe, Johann Wolfgang von (1809/1994) *Elective Affinities. Translated by David Constantine*. Oxford: Oxford University Press.

Haddon, Mark (2003) *The Curious Incident of the Dog in the Night-time*. London: Jonathan Cape.

Heaney, Seamus (1996) *Crediting Poetry*. Oldcastle: The Gallery Press.

Herbert, W. and Hollis, Matthew (eds) (2000) *Strong Words: Modern Poets on Modern Poetry*. Northumberland: Bloodaxe Books.

Hollinghurst, Alan (2004) *The Line of Beauty*. London: Picador.

Hyde, Lewis (2008) *Trickster Makes This World*. Edinburgh: Canongate.

James, Henry (1915/1984) *Letters*, Vol. iv, ed. Leon Edel. London: Macmillan.

Jekyll, Gertrude (1995) *Colour in the Flower Garden*. London: Reed.

Joyce, James (1916/2000) *A Portrait of the Artist as a Young Man*. London: Penguin Classics.

K, Oscar and Karrebaek, Dorte (2011) *The Camp (Lejren)*. Denmark: Høst & søn.

Kafka, Franz (1925/1994) *The Trial*. London: Penguin Books.

Kott, Jan (1974) *Shakespeare Our Contemporary*, USA, Norton Library.

Kundera, Milan (1986/2005) *The Art Of The Novel*. London: Faber and Faber.

Mantel, Hilary (2009) *Wolf Hall*. London: Fourth Estate.

Masefield, John (1935/2000) *The Box of Delights*, London: Egmont Books.

Mitchell, David (2001) *number9dream*. London: Sceptre.

Mitchell, David (2004) *Cloud Atlas*. London: Hodder and Stoughton.

Nicholls, David (2009) *One Day*. London: Hodder and Stoughton.

O'Neill, Joseph (2009) *Netherland*. London: Harper Perennial.

Orwell, George (1937/2001) *The Road To Wigan Pier*. London: Penguin Books.

Orwell, George (1945/1969) *Animal Farm*. London: Penguin Books.

Orwell, George (1945/2000) 'In Defence of PG Wodehouse', Bernard Crick (ed.) *George Orwell: Essays*. London: Penguin Classics.

Orwell, George (1946/2000) 'Why I Write', in Bernard Crick (ed.) *George Orwell: Essays*. London: Penguin Classics.

Ouseby, Jack (1992) 'Reading and The Imagination', in Martin Coles and Colin Harrison (eds) *The Reading for Real Handbook*. London: Routledge.

Plock, Vike Martina (2012) 'Sartorial Connections: Fashion, Clothes, and Character in Elizabeth Bowen's To the North', *Modernism/Modernity* 19(2).

Prose, Francine (2006) *Reading Like A Writer*. New York: Harper Perennial.

Quiller-Couch, Arthur (1919) *The Oxford Book of English Verse: 1250–1900*. Oxford: Oxford University Press.

Rice, Ben (2002) *Pobby and Dingan*. London: Vintage.

Sacks, Oliver (1985/2007) *The Man Who Mistook His Wife For a Hat*. London: Picador.

Santoro, Laura (2008) *Mercy*. London: Portobello Books.

Shields, Carol (1993/2008) *The Stone Diaries*. London: Harper Perennial.

Slim, Field Marshall Sir William (1956) *Defeat Into Victory*. London: Cassell and Company.

Sinha, Indra (2007) *Animal's People*. London: Simon and Schuster.

Smiley, Jane (2006) *13 Ways of Looking At The Novel*. London: Faber and Faber.

Tennyson, Alfred (1850/2008) *In Memoriam A. H. H.* Gloucester: Dodo Press.

Waugh, Evelyn (1948) 'Felix Culpa', *Commonweal* (16 July): 323.

Weimann, Robert (1967/1978) *Shakespeare and the Popular Tradition in the Theater*. Baltimore, MD: The John Hopkins University Press.

Woolf, Virginia (2004) *A Passionate Apprentice: The Early Journals 1897-1909*. London: Pimlico.

Conferences and Seminars

Lynn, David (2009) Seminar, University of Exeter, 2 March.

Pullman, Philip (2010) 'The Borderland', paper presented at the University of Exeter, 20 January.

Some Further Reading

Reading Like A Writer by Francine Prose, Harper Perennial
13 Ways of Looking At The Novel by Jane Smiley, Faber and Faber
On Writing by Jorge Luis Borges, Penguin Books
The Art of Fiction by Henry James, BiblioBazaar
Not Knowing, The Essays and Interviews by Donald Barthelme, Counterpoint
Preparation of The Novel by Roland Barthes, Columbia University Press
The Art of Fiction by David Lodge, Penguin
Writing Fiction: A Guide to Narrative Craft by Janet Burroway, Elizabeth Stuckey-French and Ned Stuckey-French, Pearson
Consciousness and the Novel by David Lodge, Penguin
How Fiction Works by James Wood, Vintage
A Passion for Narrative by Jack Hodkins, McClelland & Stewart
Anatomy of Criticism by Northrop Frye, Princeton University Press
Is There A Book In You? by Alison Baverstock, A C Black
The Art of the Novel by Milan Kundera
On Writing: A Memoir of the Craft by Stephen King, Hodder and Stoughton
Aspects of the Novel by E. M. Forster, Penguin Classics
Steering the Craft by Ursula K. Le Guin, Eighth Mountain Press
Liar's Landscape by Malcolm Bradbury, Picador
Out of Sheer Rage by Geoff Dyer, Abacus
Becoming a Writer by Dorothea Brande, Jeremy P. Tarcher
The 3 am Epiphany by Brian Kitely, Writers Digest Books
Imaginative Writing: The Elements of Craft by Janet Burroway, Penguin
Writing Down The Bones by Natalie Goldberg, Shambhala Publications

How to Write a Novel by John Braine, Methuen

'Get A Real Degree' (an article in the *LRB* by Elif Batuman, available on-line)

How Not to Write a Novel by Sandra Newman and Howard Mittelmark

You Talkin' To Me? Rhetoric from Aristotle to Obama by Sam Leith, Profile Books

Talking About Detective Fiction by P. D. James, Faber and Faber

Six Memos for the Next Milennium by Italo Calvino, Penguin

The Creative Writing Coursebook, ed. Julia Bell and Paul Magrs, Macmillan

INDEX